From an unfinished pencil sketch by Wentworth _ the only portrait taken of the Poet.

John G. C. Brainard

BRAINARD.
EPITHALAMIUM
POEMS AND MEMOIR.
1842.

THE

POEMS

OF

JOHN G. C. BRAINARD.

A

NEW AND AUTHENTIC COLLECTION,

WITH AN ORIGINAL

MEMOIR OF HIS LIFE.

HARTFORD:
S. ANDRUS & SON.
MDCCCXLVI.

ADVERTISEMENT.

THE first edition of the poems of Brainard appeared during the lifetime of the author, (1825,) and embraced nearly one half of the poetry contained in the present volume. That edition was revised by him; and, as some of the lines differ materially from the copy originally published in the Connecticut Mirror, it may be interesting to those familiar with his writings to compare them. A few of these alterations will be found in the addenda, and a single instance may be noticed, in comparing the facsimile in this volume with the revised copy.

A second edition was published in 1832, and an addition was made to the contents of the previous one of about fifty pieces, which had appeared chiefly in the Mirror after the Spring of 1825. The mechanical execution and general appearance of that volume were unfavorable; and in these respects it was not congenial to the tastes of the lovers of poetry generally, or satisfactory to the numerous friends of the bard. It was also, for the most part, printed in the absence of the publisher, a fact which may account for many of the numerous errors, chiefly in orthography and punctuation, which often marred the beauties, and obscured the sentiment of the poet. Beside these faults, the volume contained several pieces which, it is ascertained, were not the productions of the muse of Brainard. Among these were the pieces entitled, "The Young Widow," "O well I love thee, native Land," "To the Moon, a Fragment," "Good Night," "The Girl I love," "To an antique Female Bust," and "To mine Old Plaid Cloak." All these pieces are from the pens of gentlemen better known in other walks than those of poesy; yet there is in them so much of poetic excellence, and of affinity with Brainard, that in their former association with his poetry they harmonized finely. They both gave and received beauty in their contact — a fact highly complimentary, both to our poet and to the authors of these now "rejected pieces"; the last of which, especially, though by a different author, is characteristic not only of Brainard, but also of *his* "Old Plaid Cloak."

During the preparation of the present volume for the press, exertions made to discover any unpublished poetry of the author have availed but little; this is the less surprising, when it is considered that probably every occasional production of his found its way, almost immediately, into the columns of a newspaper. One or two pieces, however, with a few others from the files of the Mirror, are now first published in a collection of his poetry. The arrangement by the author of the first half of the poems — that published under his supervision and ending with "The Two Comets," is retained in the present edition, with the exception of two or three of the pieces above referred to, and the opening poem, "On Connecticut River"; — and those which follow "The Two Comets" appear, generally, in the order in which they were originally published in the Mirror. The poem addressed to Charity, was the last contribution of Brainard to the columns of that paper; and as it was intended for, and appeared as the "New-Year's Verses" for 1828, the author gave it the quaint title of "Thoughts of Mr. Eli Shepard, Carrier of the Connecticut Mirror, on Charity." The errors in the former edition, before adverted to, have been corrected in the present one; and every effort has been made to present to the reader a complete and correct edition of the poetry of Brainard, and in a dress appropriate and becoming to his muse. A new Memoir of the author, more extended and fuller than any which has preceded it, has been prepared expressly for this edition; and the portrait, although from an unfinished pencil sketch, by Wentworth, (the only one known to have been taken of Brainard,) with the facsimile of his writing, it is believed will be favorably appreciated and valued by those who were familiar with the poet, and by the admirers of his genius.

THE PUBLISHER.

CONTENTS.

MEMOIR.

MEMOIR.

THE birthplace of John Gardner Calkins Brainard was New London, in Connecticut. From the period of his birth, which occurred October 21st, 1796, to the year of his entrance into college, his time was spent under the roof of his father, the Hon. Jeremiah G. Brainard, formerly a judge of the Superior Court in that State. Here he received that early culture in mind and disposition, the happy development of which since, has imparted so much pleasure to the reading community. Those habits of good-nature, modesty, and sociableness, as also those poetic tastes and sensibilities, by which he became distinguished, were doubtless nurtured by his favorable circumstances, during that important period of life. Having finished his preparatory studies under the direction of an elder brother, he entered Yale College in 1811. He is described by those who knew him then, as not having made such efforts in the character of a student, as might have been expected from his evident genius and capacity. Whether this fact had its foundation in a native inactivity of body and mind, in too humble an appreciation of his powers, or in the generous sensibility which cannot inflict pain on a rival, it is difficult to determine. Probably these several circumstances had each its influence. The regard which was entertained by his fellow students for his superior intellect, — his beautiful genius, — doubtless became the more enhanced, on this account. Neither envy, nor the dread of rivalry, forbade the admiration of talent which interfered not with the honors of others, but was contented with its own manifestations, in its own way. That which he possessed of the *mens divinior*, was calmly and unostentatiously evolved on every occasion. It acquired character and consistency by degrees, and resembled the flowing of his own *Connecticut*, noiseless and placid and full, rather than the leaping and foaming of a cataract. His social and convivial qualities, equally with the gifts of intellect, drew forth the strong regards of his more particular acquaintance in the college, and he met them with the smile and the repartee, — with the playful jest and mimic fun, which are so easily tolerated in the gayer intercourse of friends, and which, in him, never gave offence. The possession of feelings of this kind was not, however, incompatible with a tinge of thoughtful and almost depressing pensiveness, which was sometimes observed to steal over his features.

Brainard graduated in 1815, and on his return to his native place, commenced the study of law, in the office of his brother, William F. Brainard, Esq. On the completion of his professional course and admission to the Bar, he removed to the city of Middletown, with a view to the practice of law. This was in 1819, but in the earlier part of the year 1822, we find him in the city of Hartford, engaged in the duties of an editor of a weekly paper, the "*Connecticut Mirror*."* His career in the profession he had first chosen was, therefore, short. He seems neither to have been fitted for the law, nor the law for him. The dreams of fancy filled his soul, when he should have been adding to the mass of his legal learning. He beckoned to the muses, when he should have secured a client. He cherished an over-wrought sensibility, when he should have ventured the asperity of the world's men and the world's ways. In short he considered himself as possessing "a temperament," to use his own words,

* These duties commenced on the 25th of February.

" much too sensitive for his own comfort, which exposed him to personal altercation, contradiction, and that sharp collision which tries and strengthens the passions of the heart, at least as much as it does the faculties of the mind." We can scarcely wonder, then, that he was not destined to excel in a calling, which requires a hardy cast of character, and which leads into those paths of strife, ambition, and political distinction, so abhorred by the fond poetic enthusiast. With whatever gifts of intellect he was endowed, and however he might have excelled in his profession, had he applied all his powers to it; still it was not the calling he loved, and he had no disposition to make the required application. Judging by the event, he was destined to become eminent in another walk of life. The temperaments and the tastes of men are originally different, one from another. God has made them, by their mental and physical structure, for particular spheres of exertion, thus giving a beautiful variety to human existence, and to the pursuits of men. Some are formed to occupy one department of his earthly providence, and others an entirely different one. Cowper could no more be a lawyer or public man, when he was made and *preconfigured* for a poet, than the individual we once heard of was destined to be a poet, who was able to compose but a single couplet in all his life, and that only in the unconscious hours of sleep. Let not then the providence of God be arraigned, by which each one will

> . . . . . "fall
> Just in the niche he was ordained to fill."

The direction of Brainard's genius appeared in the poetic creations which he was meditating, during his residence in Middletown. These resulted in several of his smaller printed poems. He also prepared, at the same period, several pieces for a literary paper, conducted by Cornelius Tuthill, Esq., one of the earlier editors of the "Christian Spectator." The paper was published at New Haven, and called "The Microscope." The humorous story of Gabriel Gap, in that publication, was from the pen of Brainard, though he left it unfinished.

The profession of law was thus abandoned for the no less trying, and far more precarious career, of the literary adventurer. But the latter was the pursuit of his choice, and though he seemed not to have any brilliant anticipations at the commencement, he attained to a distinction which only sterling talents could have commanded. For a portion of his task as an editor of a weekly newspaper, it has been supposed that neither his temper, nor his training, was fitted. It is true that he had no fondness for political asperity and wrangling. For such times he was not born, unless possibly to allay them, by his pacific and candid spirit. He could not with comfort to himself mingle in the din of such a controversy. But it may well be questioned, whether too slight an estimate has not sometimes been put upon his capacity, to conduct the editorial department of such a journal as he undertook, even in its political discussions. The character of the matter which actually appeared in "The Mirror," is not, in every case, the true test of his ability. He was capable of greater originality of thought, and comprehensiveness of views, on the topics alluded to, than the first naked aspect of things would indicate. We are assured by competent testimony, that labored and able political articles were withheld from publication, owing to causes over which he had little control. It is not, perhaps, necessary to detail the facts, but they certainly go far to exculpate him from the charge of levity, or weakness, in conducting the editorial department of his paper. Prudential considerations were suffered to have sway, at the expense of his reputation for political tact and foresight. The only substitutes for the articles referred to, were such brief and tame pieces as he could prepare, after the best and almost only hours for composition had passed by. This circumstance, together with the consciousness that the paper was ill sustained in respect to its patronage, was sufficiently discouraging to a person, whose sensibilities were as acute as those of Brainard's. It accounts also for the frequent turns of mental depression which marked his latter years, — heightened, indeed, by that frequent and mortifying concomitant of genius, — slender pecuniary means.

In whatever pertained to the literary portion of his paper, he was certainly at home. Hence his notices of new works were interesting and able. He possessed the urbanity and frankness to give utterance to his sense of intellectual beauty, whenever he perceived any traces of it in the authors on whom he commented. In the language of Mr. Whittier, who appreciated his character in this particular, with the kindred temper of a poet and a philanthropist: "there was too much gentleness in his nature, too much charity for the offending, and too much modesty in his own pretensions, to allow any rudeness of criticism, or severity of censure. His writings in the "Connecticut Mirror," are uniformly gentlemanly and good natured. It is impossible to discover in them any thing like malice or wantonness of satire. He was the first to award due praise to his literary brethren. His criticisms were those of a man willing to lend his fine ear to the harmonies of poetry, and his clear, healthful eye to the light of intellectual beauty, wherever these were to be seen or heard.

Of his poetic pieces in "The Mirror," there was but one opinion. They were well received, and deserved the tribute of praise which was accorded by many a reader. The reputation which he earned was not, however, instantaneous. He at first became a favorite in a circle of friends, and by them his talents were known and somewhat appreciated. Still, the impression which he was calculated to make on their minds, was not fully felt, until certain poems of a superior order came out. The lines "On the birthday of Washington," beginning

"Behold the mossed cornered-stone dropped from the wall"

and some others, burst on their view, like brilliant meteors, surprising and enchanting them. After this, it was not long before he was honored by the literary part of the community generally, and by all who took an interest in the productions of native genius; and every number of "The Mirror" was seized with avidity by men, women, and children, to see if it contained any of Brainard's poetry. It is on these poetic effusions that his claims to the regard of future times will principally rest. For however happy he may have been in several of his prose compositions, the public know him mostly as a poet, and in that light will he here be chiefly viewed. The few criticisms which we shall attempt in respect to his poetry will appear in the sequel. In this part of our task, our only design was to present the few incidents of his life, and sketch the striking points of his general character.

We have already seen Brainard in the commencement of his literary career, as an editor, and as a writer of poetry. Short as that career was, extending only to six years, it was nevertheless important to his own fame, and to his country's intellectual wealth. He seems to have availed himself of his opportunities for observation to good effect, and was not unversed in the learning of books. He culled every variety of sweet that lay in his path, and looked on nature and man, with the eye of a poet, and to subserve a poet's purposes. All our real bards, men renowned in song, have proved themselves to be men of knowledge. Those undying forms of thought which they put forth, are the products of capacious, well-stored, far-reaching intellects. They may not be all scholars, in the rigid and collegiate sense of the word, but they are men of information and intellectual power. That which they write is stamped with the seal of truth and adherence to nature, and shows the vestiges of study and research of some kind. Thus Brainard had his rich intellectual acquisitions ; but they were not gathered in the ordinary way of the student, ever bending over his books, and observing nightly vigils. He was " one of those men, who," as a friend that well knew him remarked, "love to lie on their backs, and *see* what they can *think*." Brainard acquired his rich and beautiful intellectual stores somewhat in this manner. And he had frequent occasion to lay them under contribution, in the preparation of poems for his paper. These pieces, as already remarked, were eagerly read, and highly commended. They established his fame as a poet, and drew him forth from the retirement which he seemed to love so well. Praise, however, apparently excites no emotions of vanity in his bosom, and he ever retired thither for the sweetest solace he found or desired on earth. Several of the pieces, however, as they were composed in the hurry, and under the embarrassments incident to his profession as an editor, received less care and polish than should have been bestowed upon them, but they all showed a ready and skilful hand, and that only leisure was wanting to their perfection. Negligence, in some instances, was but too natural under these circumstances, and taste could not always be consulted or indulged.

Three years sufficed to furnish a small volume of the poetry thus contributed to "The Mirror," or that remained by him unprinted. It was published early in the year 1825. It was accompanied by a very brief and unpretending introduction, and left to find its way by its own merits, into the hearts and minds of his countrymen.* The *naïveté* with which it was commit-

* The Introduction to the volume was as follows: — "The author of the following pieces has been induced to publish them in a book, from considerations which cannot be interesting to the public. Many of these little poems have been printed in the *Connecticut Mirror;* and others are just fit to keep them company. No apologies are made, and no criticisms deprecated. The commonplace story of the importunities of friends, though it had its share in the publication, is not insisted upon; but the vanity of the author, if others choose to call it such, is a natural motive, and the hope of 'making a little something by it,' is an honest acknowledgment, if it is a poor excuse." The motto of the title-page was as quaint, —

"Some said, 'John print it;' others said 'Not so;'
Some said 'It might do good;' others said 'No.'"

Bunyan's Apology.

ted to their attention, was answered by a generous and general approval of its contents. Our ablest periodical literature, in one instance at least,* spoke in tones of approbation and encouragement, stating, however, such exceptions to their general good opinion, as judicious criticism is always expected to put forth. No other literary effort followed the preparation of this volume, except other fugitive pieces, which, together with the former, were collected in a volume published in 1832, by Mr. Goodsell.

But the voice of the bard was destined ere long to be hushed in the silence of death. Prematurely was he called (we speak with deference to the divine arrangements,) to resign life with all its sweets and its fame, into the hand of the Giver. His health had begun to decline previously to the spring of 1827, at which period he retired from his professional labors, though not with a design to relinquish them finally. He sought repose in his native town, where the assiduities of friendship and affection, so grateful in sickness and depression, were bestowed and enjoyed, in a high degree. But nothing could arrest the progress of the disease with which he was visited. It proved

* North American Review.

to be consumption, that surest precursor of death, though often slow in its work, and flattering in its symptoms. Resort was had in summer to a short residence on Long Island. No material relief, however, was afforded by the excursion, and he was forced to abandon the idea of returning to Hartford, and resuming the duties of editorship. He lingered till the 26th of September the following year, (1828,) when he cheerfully departed to his rest. During this period of physical debility and decay, he exerted, as usual, his mental powers in the composition of several short, but beautiful poems, which were published in "The Mirror." The circumstances of his sickness and death were detailed at the time by the Rev. Mr. M'Ewen, pastor of the church to which Brainard belonged, in a letter to the Rev. Dr. Hawes, of Hartford. We adopt it from Mr. Whittier's "Sketch of Brainard's Life" prefixed to Goodsell's edition of his "Literary Remains."

"In my first visit to him, two or three months before his death, he said: 'I am sick and near death, and I ought not to be too confident how I should act or feel had I a prospect of health and the worldly pleasures and prosperity which it would offer. But if I know myself I would, were I well, devote my life to the service of Jesus Christ.' I stated some of the main doctrines of Christianity. 'These are Scripture,' he said, 'they are true and delightful to me. The plan of salvation in the Gospel is all that I wish for; — it fills me with wonder and gratitude; and makes the prospect of death not only peaceful but joyful. My salvation,' he continued, 'is not to be effected by a profession of religion; but when I read Christ's requirements, and look round on my friends and acquaintances, I cannot be content without performing this public duty.' He was propounded, and in due time, pale and feeble, yet manifestly with mental joy and serenity, he came to the house of God, professed his faith and was baptized and entered into covenant with God and his people. The next Sabbath the Lord's Supper was administered. It was wet, and he could not be out. His disappointment was great. A few friends went to his room and communed with him there in this ordinance. While his father's family and others, during the scene, were dissolved in tears, he sat with dignity and composure, absorbed in the interesting ceremony in which he was engaged. In my last interview with him, after he was, at his own request, left alone with me, he said: 'I wish not to be deceived about my state, — but I am not in the usual condition to try myself. No one abuses a sick man, — every thing around me in sympathy and kindness. I used to be angry when people spoke what was true of me. I have now no resentment. I can forgive all and pray, I think, for the salvation of all. I am not tried with pain. I have hardly any outward trial.' 'But,' said I, 'you have one great trial, — you must soon part with life:' 'And I am willing,' he replied. 'The Gospel makes my prospect delightful. God is a God of truth, and I think I am reconciled to him.' I saw him no more, but was told that he died in peace."

It may be interesting to learn a few other particulars respecting the poet, during his last illness. To this end, we are happy to have it in our power to introduce a short account, furnished by a gentleman in Hartford, a friend and acquaintance of Brainard's, who called on him, eight or ten days before the death of the latter. This gentleman had previously written him during his sickness, and accompanied the letter by a copy of "Wolfe's Remains." We give the account as it was detailed in conversation.

"I called at Judge Brainard's, and on inquiry for John was shown unannounced into his room, or rather the parlour where he was, — and not expecting to find him there. Of course both parties were taken by surprise. Brainard was sitting in the middle of the room, dressed in his usual attire, and with his hat on and his cane near by. In his lap, was a large old-fashioned family Bible lying open, in the reading of which he was entirely absorbed, and from which his attention was withdrawn only by my entrance. Immediately after his recognition of me, and the usual greeting, he said ' he had received the letter which I had addressed to him, with the accompanying volume which had been to him like a draught of water to a thirsty man.' He then almost immediately spoke of his religious views and feelings, — apologizing for his seeming abruptness in introducing the topic of religion, by a reference to his then feeble condition, (he could speak only in a whisper,) and to the opinion now entertained by him, that this was 'the only subject.' Pointing to the Bible, he spoke of the great comfort and support he there found, and with much earnestness expressed his confident hope, that not only myself, but also his other familiar friends at Hartford, would 'get right,' and derive from that book the same consolation which it now afforded him. He said he suffered no bodily pain,* — none worthy of a thought; — that he had no apprehen-

* The impression of the family was, that he had, at times, suffered much. If so, his religious views, hopes, and aspirations had probably rendered him superior to the usual distressing accompaniments of disease.

sion of death, — that he indeed longed, and was impatient to depart. In expressing a wish for an early dismissal from life, he desired to avoid a sinful impatience, — but that the earliest time, so that it was God's time, would be to him most welcome. I gathered from his remarks, that his time was divided between his *Bible* and the thoughts and meditations it inspired, and the *garden* where he occasionally sat, and breathed the fresh air. His sister, who, on my entrance, had cautioned me not to let her brother become exhausted by too much conversation, here, for the second or third time, appeared at the door of the apartment, with so much anxiety depicted on her countenance, that her solicitude could not be mistaken nor disregarded, notwithstanding the earnest wish manifested by her brother (who now for the first and only time spoke aloud) that my stay might be prolonged. Fearing, therefore, the effect on him of a longer interview, I here took my leave; and a short week or two brought Brainard the release from life, which he so earnestly desired."

In joining the church, as narrated by Mr. M'Ewen above, it may be added, as we learn, that Brainard being too feeble to go to church and remain through the ordinary services, consequently arrived at and entered the sanctuary, when these were nearly or quite through. Every one present (literally, almost,) knew him, — the occasion of his coming was understood, — and when he appeared, pale, feeble, emaciated, and trembling in consequence of his extreme debility, the sensation it produced was at once apparent throughout the whole assembly. There seemed to be an instinctive homage paid to the grace of God in him; or perhaps the fact shows, how readily a refined Christian community sympathizes with genius and virtue destined to an early tomb.

The lively grief of the reading community, as well as of his friends in particular, attested their sense of the loss which had been experienced. He had evidently been regarded with great favor, and it was no unnatural feeling to dwell, with fond pensiveness, on the memory of one who had often contributed to their serious and innocent gratification. Thus he shone among the

> "Bright forms we sorrowing weep,
> So fleet they passed away to die,"

and the lovers of song had only the mournful satisfaction of expressing their regard for departed excellence. His death was extensively lamented, and many felt that one had fallen who had already achieved not a little, and promised still more, in his devotion to a delightful art.

Several traits of Brainard's character have incidentally appeared already; but we should do him injustice not to give more prominence to a few of its features. His mind, naturally tender and susceptible in a high degree, was given to pensive thought; and in his riper years its developments amounted at times, to melancholy and depression. Whether this is to be attributed to a cause which has been publicly stated,—a cause which often withers the affections of the young heart, —we know not. If that cause existed, it was unknown to his immediate relatives. But whatever may have been the occasion of the characteristic we speak of, the latter was an acknowledged reality, and even in his poetry itself, the tones of a deeply sad spirit often break forth. The "Edinburgh Review," in one instance, attaches to this character of his poetry, the epithets of "melancholy" and "wayward," and quotes as an example, the touching stanzas beginning with the line

> "The dead leaves strew the forest walk."

A friend and admirer of the poet remarked to us, that he appeared as one, who, notwithstanding the frequent gayety of his strains, " was disposed to sport with his own feelings." The sadness which he felt within could not be better thrown off, or parried, than by indulging in an external gayety. Still there were bright sunny spots in his life, an innocent joyousness was not an entire stranger to his bosom, and even immersed, as he often was, in dark and sombre thoughts, he never became moody and misanthropic. In the language of another, "disheartened and despondent as we know Brainard was, looking out upon the world with an eye that saw every thing glowing with prismatic beauty, yet mournfully feeling that this beauty was not made for him, — still, when he met a friend, the cloud passed instantly from his brow, a smile was on his lips, and words of merriment and levity broke from his tongue. It was apparent that for the moment, he obtained relief from his painful musings in the play of a humorous fancy, — a laugh seemed to beguile his sorrow, — a joke to scare back into their recesses, the demons that preyed upon his bosom. Those only, who knew him well, can understand how interesting was this light of his mind, breaking out amid the clouds and darkness which encompassed it." We may add to the above, that he possessed a keen perception of the humorous and ridiculous, — that he had the art of seizing on those points of character in others, which constituted their foibles, as well as their excellences, — that his mode of expression, like the association of his ideas, was at once singular and engaging, — and hence on these several accounts, he could inspire in the minds of a circle, emotions of mirth and gayety, apparently the most opposite to those, with which his own mind was so frequently occupied.

It is not surprising, then, that he was eminently formed for society, and the enjoyment of its innocent festivities and delights, notwithstanding the retiring modesty and the keen sensitiveness by which he was distinguished. "His habits of self-reliance," says Mr. Whittier, "of a gentle retirement into the calm beauty of his own mind, rendered him, in a measure, indifferent to the opinion of the world. Yet he loved society, — the society of the gifted and intellectual, — and of those who had become accustomed to his peculiarities of manner and feeling, who could appreciate his merit, or relish his good-natured jests, and 'mocks, and knaveries,' and laugh with him at what he considered the ludicrous eagerness of the multitude after the vanities of existence. In larger and mixed circles, his peculiar sensitiveness was a frequent cause of unhappiness. Amidst his gayety and humor, a word spoken inadvertently, — some unmeaning gesture, — some casual inattention or unlucky oversight checked at once the free flow of his sprightly conversation, — the jest died upon his lips, — and the melancholy which had been lifted from his heart, fell again with increased heaviness."

There was a quiet sportiveness and humor about Brainard, which rendered him a highly agreeable companion, and threw a charm over the circles in which he visited. It arose at times into wit of a keen and brilliant character. This, his writings also sufficiently show. It is no matter of surprise that he was a favorite in company, or peculiarly interesting in conversation, to his intimate friends. We have heard of specimens of his lively and facetious turn, one of which we will take the liberty to record. In his native place, we believe it was, he attended, on some occasion, a meeting which was successively addressed by two preachers, who claimed to be divinely moved, in the exercise of their gifts. The first one was brief, and in what he said seemed to defer to his brother, as more likely to fulfil the expectations of the audience. The other attempted much more, but proceeded with difficulty. Indeed, he several times offered the apology, in rather quaint phrase, that *his mind was imprisoned.*

At the close of the services, as the people retired, it was natural that the conversation should turn on the speakers. It was observed by one, that the latter preacher succeeded but indifferently. "You know," replied a by-stander, "that he complained of the imprisonment of his mind." At this moment Brainard came up, and, on hearing the conversation, remarked, in his ready and piquant manner, that "the preacher's mind might have easily *sworn out.*" The readiness of his wit was apparent in his writings, a single instance of which we will adduce. The following appears in "The Mirror" of July 5, 1824, as a retort upon one of his critics. "We observe a criticism in the 'Village Record,' on some verses headed 'The Deep,' in which the writer says, 'the word *brine* has no more business in sentimental poetry, than a pig in a parlour.' We suspect the writer, though his piece is dated Philadelphia, lives at a greater distance from the sea; and has got his ideas of the *salt water from his father's pork barrel.*"

The seeming severity, as well as the wit of the above stricture reminds us to say, that such was not the tone which he held generally towards the criticisms bestowed upon his pieces. He submitted to just and candid remarks upon his performances, with perfect good-nature. As this was a striking trait of his character, connected with his humble opinion of his own performances, it deserves some illustration. In a communication to "The Mirror" of Nov. 10, 1828, by a Lady, the writer says, — "It is too often the fault of authors that they are unwilling to submit to criticism, — still less to the alterations of others. That the subject of this article (Brainard) was superior to this, and diffident of his own abilities, appears in a letter to the (then) editor of 'The Mirror,' Mr. Lincoln, dated Jan. 1822, in which Brainard says, 'I received yours this morning, and in reading it, had to regret that you should have found it necessary to offer the slightest apology, on account of the very proper and necessary alterations in the lines I sent you. For, if I remember right, you was not only authorized, but requested to make such use of them, as would best answer the purposes of "The Mirror." From the solemn tone of your letter, I feared you was a hypochondriac, or that you was not so well acquainted with me as I could wish. Why, my dear Lincoln, when you was about it, did you not apologize for thinking me a conceited fool, who knows his verses are none of the best, and yet quarrels with his friend for coming to the same conclusion. Upon my word, I did not expect to see so much of them printed as I found in your last Mirror.' " The writer adds, — "There is something which makes us feel, as if it were almost sacrilege to bring forward to the public, what was only designed for the private eye of friendship, but it also seems as if the public had a kind of property in the private thoughts of men of genius; and when we find talents united with modesty, and good-humor, we are constrained to love, when we before admired."

In respect to other features of his character, we have the authority of a writer in the "Boston Statesman," of 1828, (as quoted by Mr. Whittier,) a gentleman intimately acquainted with the poet, who cleverly observes as follows. "Brainard did not make much show in the world. He was an unassuming and unambitious man, — but he had talents which should have made him our pride. They were not showy or dazzling, — and perhaps that is the reason that the general eye did not rest upon him, — but he had a keen discriminating susceptibility, and a taste exquisitely refined and true. . . . . . Brainard had no enemies. It was not that his character was negative, or his courtesy universal. There was a directness in his manner, and a plain-spoken earnestness in his address, which could never have been wanting in proper discrimination. He would never have compromised with the unworthy for their good opinion. But it was his truth, — his fine, open, ingenuous truth, — bound up with a character of great purity and benevolence, which won love for him. I never met a man of whom all men spoke so well. I fear I never shall. When I was introduced to him he took me aside and talked with me for an hour. I shall never forget that conversation. He made no commonplace remarks. He would not talk of himself, though I tried to lead him to it. He took a high intellectual tone, and I never have heard its beauty or originality equalled. He knew wonderfully well the secrets of mental relish and development; and had evidently examined himself till he had grown fond, as every one must who does it, of a quiet, contemplative, self-cultivating life." But, however his habitual aspirations may have been after this refined enjoyment, he still greatly delighted in the visible and palpable of human life. In whatever manner these different traits may be reconciled, or accounted for, as meeting in the same subject, yet it is certain that no man ever enjoyed more than he did the every-day bustle of the world. He loved to mix with it, and in it, and cared not if he was borne along, for a time, in its current. A brigade review, with its exhilarating sights, sounds, and cheer, seemed to give him, in company with a few friends, as unsophisticated a feeling of pleasure, as it did to the veriest boy on the ground.

The writer above quoted, notices the poet in his social hours. "The first time I ever saw him, I met him in a gay and fashionable circle. He was pointed out to me as the poet Brainard. A plain, ordinary looking individual, careless in his dress, and apparently without the least outward claim to the attention of those who value such advantages. But there was no person there, so much or so flatteringly attended to. He was among those who saw him every day and knew him familiarly; and I almost envied him, as he went round, the unqualified kindness and even affection, with which every bright girl and every mother in the room received him. He was evidently the idol, not only of the poetry loving and gentler sex, — but also of the young men who were about him, — an evidence of worth, let me say, which is as high as it is uncommon."

The susceptibility and benevolence of his heart, were apparent to the view of all who were acquainted with him. To illustrate his character, in this respect, we are happy to furnish the following from a manuscript which has been put into our hands, drawn up by an intimate friend of the poet. "I have several times," he says, "attempted it," (that is, to portray the character of Brainard,) "either for my own amusement, or the gratification of others, and have succeeded only in sketching a sort of panegyric of any amiable, talented, and refined gentleman. Still he was a man of many distinctive characteristics. They were those traits, however, which pleased by their beauty, rather than astonished by their obtrusive boldness. Indeed, his governing quality, and that which mellowed the light and shade of all the rest, was a *delicate sensibility*. It was not, however, that morbid susceptibility to malevolent impressions, which some cultivate for effect, — a compound of sullenness and misanthropy, — a malignant excrescence, that deforms all the beautiful proportions which the soul brought from the hands of its Creator; but it was the offspring of benevolence rather, which delighted in the happiness, and was pained by the misery of any sentient being in the universe. It is true it could ill bear the shocks to which it was exposed in this jostling and selfish world; but it rarely led him to murmur at the causes of his own unhappiness, or excited hostility against the authors of ill to him. He bore his own griefs in silence, whatever they were, but was aroused to active sympathy whenever he saw his fellow-man, or even a brute suffer." . . . . .

"I first met him while he resided in Middletown. I accompanied a sister of mine, while making an afternoon call on Miss S———, who, you know, was somewhat celebrated for her beauty and wit. There were several ladies in the room when we entered. Brainard was there, the soul and spirit of the conversation. He seemed delighted, and was in his happiest mood. Of course none present could fail to be delighted in him. Through awkwardness, or some other cause, I had taken a seat somewhat by myself, and being much younger than the rest, was very naturally neglected. The embarrassment of my situation did not long escape the observation of Brainard. He left the circle of beauty and brilliant conversation, and in the kindest and most affectionate manner addressed to me such conversation as was calculated to please one of my age. You may be sure I was interested. It was not long before he was again the centre of attraction, and his benevolent face lighted up with peculiar joy when he found my embarrassment removed, and me a sharer in the conversation of that pleasant circle of friends. Still, he did not neglect me, nor would he allow others to do so. But by often addressing me he seemed to say, 'we may all be happy, but the ease and happiness of my young friend must not be neglected.' On parting, his cordial invitation to call on him, and make use of his hospitality while I remained in town, was fully in keeping with his kindness during our short interview. In all this there was nothing of that patronizing air, which is so commonly apparent, when men offer politeness to those younger than themselves; but just enough deference to my opinion to gratify self-love. In short, there was just that *tact* which made me feel pleased with myself, and grateful to him."

To the general beauty of his character, we add the testimony of an accomplished female author, whose representation is no less beautiful than just. We quote it from Mr. Whittier's "Sketch." "To the intellectual power and poetical eminence of Mr. Brainard, the public will undoubtedly do justice. But those who knew and valued him as a *friend*, can bear testimony to the intrinsic excellences of his character. They were admitted with a generous freedom into the sanctuary of his soul, and saw those fountains of deep and disinterested feeling which were hidden from casual observation. Friendship was not in him a modification of selfishness, lightly conceived, and as lightly dissolved. His sentiments respecting it were formed on the noble models of ancient story ; and he proved himself capable of its delicate perceptions, and its undeviating integrities. His heart had an aptitude both for its confidential interchange, and its sacred responsibilities. In his intercourse with society, he exhibited neither the pride of genius, nor the pedantry of knowledge To the critic he might have appeared deficient in personal dignity. So humbly did he think of himself, and his own attainments, that the voice of approbation and kindness seemed necessary to assure his spirits, and even to sustain his perseverance in the labors of literature. Possessed both of genuine wit, and of that playful humor which rendered his company sought and admired, he never trifled with the feelings of others, or aimed to shine at their expense. Hence he expected the same regard to his own mental comfort, and was exceedingly vulnerable to the careless jest, or to the chillness of reserve.

" It did not require the eye of intimacy to discover that he was endowed with an acute sensibility. This received early nurture and example in the bosom of most affectionate relatives. The endearing associations connected with his paternal mansion, preserved their freshness and force, long after he ceased to be an inmate there. . . . . . The efforts which he continually put forth during his intercourse with mankind, to conceal his extreme susceptibility, sometimes gave to his manners the semblance of levity. Hence he was liable to misconstruction, and a consciousness of this, by inducing occasional melancholy and seclusion, threw him still further from those sympathies for which his affectionate spirit languished. Still it cannot be said that his sensibility had a morbid tendency. It shrank, indeed, like the Mimosa, but it had no worm at its root. Its gushings forth were in admiration of the charms of nature, and in benevolence to the humblest creature ; to the poor child in the street, and to the forest bird. It had affinity with love to God, and with good-will to man. Had his life been prolonged, and he permitted to encircle with the beautiful domestic charities a household hearth of his own, the true excellences of his heart would have gained more perfect illustration. It possessed a simplicity of trusting confidence, a fulness of tender and enduring affection, which would there have found free scope and legitimate action. There he might have worn as a crown, that exquisite sensibility, which, among proud and lofty spirits, he covered as a blemish, or shrank from as a reproach. But it pleased the Almighty early to transfer him where loneliness can no longer settle as a cloud over his soul, nor the coarse enginery which earth employs jar against its harp-strings, and obstruct its melody."

The social qualities of Brainard rendered him deservedly popular. He was formed for friendship, — he had a keen relish of its pleasures, and a nice discernment of the influences by which it might be improved and perpetuated. His heart was in unison with truth, nature, and beauty. Sweet voices, glad looks, the beamings of intelligence, the throbbings of affection, home, kindred, country, the glorious creation, all gave him the purest delight, and drew responses from every chord of his heart and harp. He was ardent and devoted in his personal attachments, and it is possible that the description of the poet might occasionally be applied to him ;

> "Then must you speak
> Of one *that loved, not wisely, but too well.*"

"An affection" (we believe it is the language of Hazlitt) "indulged to excess, or carried beyond what the position of the parties, or the worth of the regarded warrants, or excited to render superfluous service, is, in the long run, destructive of its existence, and injurious to the peace of those indulging it, in other things beside love and friendship." If, occasionally, Brainard was in danger of being carried, in his attachments, beyond the boundaries of prudence, this fact only betrayed the exuberant feelings of his fond and confiding nature.

Mr. Brainard professed the hopes, as he had also studied and believed the truths, of Christianity. His sickness and death-bed scene before described, are well adapted to impress his readers on that point. The lessons of adversity and of life's trials had not been lost upon him. They softened and refined his spirit through divine grace, and prepared it, we trust, for its entrance upon a brighter sphere. The hallowing process could not but be observed with much interest. The soul's disorders through sin are remedied often by the instrumentalities of the body's sufferings. And, transformed by the Spirit of holiness into the divine image, it gathers up its energies to meet the crisis of its fate, with cheerful and blest submission to the Sovereign Disposer. Thus it was with Brainard, as it has been with other believers. They are invigorated within, as they decay without. They grow spiritual, as the body is more inert. They are made contented, as their corporeal infirmities abound. Their spirits become joyful, as their senses are rendered incapable of gratification. And *glory* is felt to be nearer, as that greatest earthly trial approaches,— the dissolution of the body. This is the paradox of a triumphing Christianity. Let none of the choice spirits of the world be left to doubt, that the Gospel can do that for them, which it did for Brainard,— which it has done for others endowed with all the gifts, and exposed to all the temptations, of genius.

The person of Brainard was somewhat below the ordinary size. The bland feelings of his heart, as well as his intelligence, beamed from his eye, as they were also expressed in the lineaments of his countenance generally. In the intercourse of friendship, and in the lively sallies of wit, his face was wont to glow with a fine expression. There was a carelessness about his personal appearance and costume,— his attitudes and walk,— which, though not obnoxious to animadversion, showed the abstractedness of the poet and the man of thought. His sensitiveness was particularly manifested by any allusion to his size. Little as such a circumstance deserved consideration or notice on his part, it was a peculiarity of the man, that he seemed to wish it had been otherwise. We should find it difficult, were we to undertake it, to account for the whims of intellectual men ; and these things are mentioned, only because the public regard any thing as interesting, which illustrates the character of a favorite.

Brainard was in the habit of rapid composition. This was in agreement with the character of his mind, and was aided by the circumstances in which he was led to write his poems. The necessity of filling some column or part of a column of his paper with verses, prompted to the composition of most of his pieces, and it was hence almost unavoidable that he should write in haste, and often in a state of mind adverse to poetical inspiration. The ease, however, with which he poured out his thoughts on paper, made some amends for this disadvantage. In any place, and in any situation, it is understood, he could give audience to the whisper of his Muse. *

* A single anecdote in illustration. A friend had long solicited Brainard to write for him a piece of poetry for the Commonplace Book of a young lady ; from which, on some plea, he had always excused himself. One wintry day he again entered the editor's room, with the identical album in hand. Brainard was shivering with cold ; there were only a few exhausted embers on the hearth, and no wood in the room. After a few moments, he turned to his friend and said ; "I tell you what : if you will run up stairs and bring me down an arm-full of wood, I 'll write for you." The wood was in

The above is the substance of what we have been able to gather of the history and character of Brainard, from published records, and from the communications of private friendship and acquaintanceship. It might be a matter of regret, that a larger number of incidents pertaining to his life, and a fuller delineation of his intellect, disposition, and habits, could not be presented in this place, were it not true, that the interest of literary biography depends but in part on the abundance of the materials thus spread out before the public eye. We look not for adventures and startling incidents, in the life of a mere poet or literary man. We can well dispense also with many offerings, in the shape of encomium, and the enthusiastic admiration of friends, to his hallowed memory. We love chiefly to contemplate him in his writings, — to learn the man

---

the garret, up two flights of stairs; but the book was handed to Brainard, and off went the friend for his burden, glad in any way to secure the poetry. He had hardly returned before Brainard had completed the beautiful lines commencing, "See to your book, young lady."

We know, also, that some portion of the lines on Connecticut River (which originally appeared as "New-Year's Verses," with the caption, "The Compliments of the Year 1827 to the Connecticut River,") went to the compositor in fragments of a few lines, *as he was waiting for copy.*

and his story there. Sometimes, when a bright and beautiful luminary has blazed in the intellectual horizon, we are disappointed, as in the case of Shakspeare, at the meagre details of the history of its course. We would trace it from its rising to its setting, and mark all its phases and variations, with the fondness of an idolatrous veneration; and satisfy our minds, how like or unlike it was, to any thing that ever attracted the view of mankind, before or since. It may also add somewhat to the admiration of genius, to be able to learn, for instance, the perilous adventures of a Camoens, swimming from a shipwreck, with his immortal epic borne in his hand above the waves, — the heroic exploits, and martyr-like sufferings, of a Cervantes in Algerine captivity, — or the wayward fortunes of a Tasso, in imprisonment, prolonged disease, and disappointed love. Still, in the majority of cases, we are contented to learn the better part of the writer in his works. Genuine talent stamps upon these its own features. The passions and dispositions of the heart stand forth embodied and living in the portraitures of the pen. There we must learn much of Brainard.

It is generally true, that excellence in any department of intellectual effort, is sooner or later recognised, on the part of those before whom it is exhibited. This is the fact in regard to poetry, perhaps, even in a greater degree, than in any other species of writing. The genuine strains of the muse readily find a response in the minds of most men. They are laid up in the memories, and rehearsed from the lips of thousands. There may, sometimes, be a tardiness in the public, as in the case of Shakspeare and Milton, in awarding its approbation; but that approbation will come at length, and make ample amends for its temporary injustice, by its increased and more lasting incense. Wherever a true bard appears, the public will become interested in him. He cannot pour forth the sweet voice of song, and long remain unheard — unanswered. Its echoes will resound through grove, and cottage, and hall — through camp and court. This is the test of worth; and it is a test to which Brainard and his poems may be confidingly committed. For although, as Snelling says, "he wrote under every disadvantage, and, as might be expected, the faults of his writings were neither few nor small," yet, "at the same time he had the stamina of poetry. Had he received encouragement sufficient to awaken his energies, his name would have lived for ever. He was wholly unconscious of his own strength, and threw off his best pieces without hesitation or premeditation. To this carelessness his faults must be attributed. In this, too, he is not alone among American poets, most of whom, it seems, write as carelessly as Brainard, though by no means as well. I wish I could mention three of them who equal John Gardiner Calkins Brainard, or six who even approach his excellence."

His poetry, it is conceived, *reflects* much of the *idiosyncrasy of the man*. His simplicity, his sportiveness, the child-like character of his feelings, the tenderness of his emotions, his humble and unpretending views of himself, and the occasional depression which came over him, are imaged forth in his poetry, as in a polished mirror. We are at no loss to decipher him, — to tell what he was. He appears honest and open as the day. Both the blossoms and the fruit of charity in him, — the elevated scriptural sentiment, and the practical purpose of good, — mingle together in varied loveliness of description, like the flowering and fruit-laden orange tree ; and while the imagination is feasted with its beauty, the heart is improved by its lessons and example of wisdom. There was no mysticism about him, — no such shaping of his words as to make men wonder what he was, and least of all, what he means. He never "minces an ambiguous skepticism," after the fashion of many of his brother bards abroad. His simple faith is simply expressed, and there is a common-sense view which he takes of man, nature, and the events of providence, that approves itself to every unsophisticated mind.

His poetry is the *expression of clear and quiet thought.* The image is brought out with distinctness, and there seems to be the absence of effort to make it dazzling and impressive. This is the true classical grace, — the repose of a pure, deep soul, as we find it in the masters of the lyre, in past times. The circumstances under which Brainard wrote, as we have already learned, precluded that degree of polish and care, so desirable in poetic composition. Hence, he has unequal poems, and sometimes careless, incorrect, or coarse lines. But he showed the natural felicity of the bard — the power of delineating in a few graceful and graphic touches, the image as it arose in his own mind. With what clearness and nature is the idea brought out in the following lines of the "Invalid"!

"The grassy lane o'er-arched with boughs and leaves,
Runs its green vista to a small bright point,
And that point is the ocean. Faint the limbs,
And all the body tires, — but for the soul
It hath its holyday in such a spot.

"A moment rest we on the only stone
In all the alley, — wipe the sweating brow,
And drop the eye upon the turf around."

The above has the terseness, the distinct thought of Cowper, and perhaps more than his simplicity. Again, in the following lines of the poem on "Connecticut River," we notice the same feature.

"Thy noble shores! where the tall steeple shines,
At mid-day, higher than thy mountain pines,
Where the white school-house with its daily drill
Of sunburnt children, smiles upon the hill;
Where the neat village grows upon the eye,
Decked forth in nature's sweet simplicity, —
Where hard-won competence, the farmer's wealth,
Gains merit, honor, and gives labor health;
Where Goldsmith's self might send his exiled band
To find a new 'Sweet Auburn,' in our land."

The name of Goldsmith here reminds us that the strain itself, as well as the theme, is not unworthy of that sweet and elegant poet.

A foreign reviewer * calls Brainard "careless," but pays him generally a high compliment, and acknowledges that, "even in this carelessness, which presents the thought in its full and undiluted form, there is often a charm." We should say, rather, that the charm lies in a certain rare union of a vivid conception with the power of graphic expression, — thus painting the idea with perfectness to the reader's mind, as in the passage on the Falls of Niagara, — which accurate and sublime

* The Edinburgh Review.

description, be it remembered, is the more remarkable from the fact that the poet never saw Niagara.

> "It would seem,
> As if God poured thee from his 'hollow hand,'
> And hung his bow upon thy awful front;
> And spoke in that loud voice, which seemed to him
> Who dwelt in Patmos for his Saviour's sake,
> 'The sound of many waters,' and had bade
> Thy flood to chronicle the ages back,
> And notch his centuries in the eternal rocks."

Also, we have the same characteristic in the lines of the "Invalid."

> "He has heard its mighty sound
> Whose bark was on its awful waters, when
> The billows swept the deck and rioted,
> Mixed with the winds round all its gallant spars.
> He too has heard its moanings, who, becalmed
> Lies like a small thing, helpless and alone,
> Upon a rolling waste immensity."

The reader of Brainard's poetry will have noticed his *nice and accurate observation of nature, and the objects around him*, so characteristic of one, who has a true poet's eye and heart. We cite the following as an example, in the "Maniac's Song"; —

> "Now I have lost my blooming health,
> And joy and hope no more abide;
> *And wildering fancies come by stealth,*
> *Like moonlight on a shifting tide.*"

Also the latter paragraph of "The Indian Summer":

"The moon stays longest for the hunter now;
The trees cast down their fruitage, and *the blithe*
And busy squirrel hoards his winter store:
While man enjoys the breeze that sweeps along
The bright blue sky above him, and that bends
Magnificently all the forest's pride,
Or whispers through the evergreens, and asks,
'What is there saddening in the autumn leaves?'"

Those associations which are suggested to the mind by natural objects, are occasionally marked by the poet, with much effect, as in the following passage;

"There 's music in the deep:—
It is not in the surf's rough roar,
Nor in the whispering shelly shore,—
They are but earthly sounds, that tell
How little of the *sea nymph's shell*
That sends its loud clear note abroad,
Or winds its softness through the flood,
Echoes through groves with coral gay,
And dies on spongy banks away."

The poem "I know a Brook," has one of those suggestive topics, which are so pleasing and instructive in poetry. After a beautiful description of the object, the poet concludes;

"There I placed
A frail memorial,—that when again
I should revisit it, the thought might come
Of the *dull tide of life,* and that *pure spring*
Which he who drinks of never shall thirst more."

The frequent occurrence of the *pathetic* in Brainard's poetry, has given it one of its most winning characteristics. Every reader feels its power, in the simple and concise touches, which could have proceeded only from a heart exquisitely alive to every holy sympathy. "Sketch of an Occurrence on board of a Brig," "On a late Loss," "The Maniac's Song," "Is it Fancy or is it Fact," are among the pieces that bear this character. Poets that excel in pathos, are not unfrequently felicitous in *humorous* description, which would appear to require talent of an opposite kind, though they may be connected by a nice and undiscernible bond. Some of the pieces of the latter kind, are "The Fragment," "Lines written for a Lady's Common-Place Book," "The Presidential Cotillion," "The Bar *versus* the Docket," and "The Two Comets." There is much genuine humor in them, though, in a few instances, they happen to contain indifferent poetry.

Our poet has a *various and appropriate manner*, in his several productions. There is in them the reverse of sameness in matter, argument, and style. Scarcely a recurrence of the same expression is found. We meet with no ever-returning identities of thought and imagery, and language. Every thing is fitted to its place and occasion; and only a natural and appropriate form seems to have been adopted, in spreading out his fancies and feelings, before the eye of the public. No one was ever less a mannerist than this poet. After reading a few pieces of some of our writers of song, you learn what to expect in regard to that which is coming, in rhythm and cadence, if not in sentiment and thought. You know the author, almost, without reading his name, as soon as a few strings of his lyre have been touched: and you have hardly the pleasure of gratifying an excited curiosity, by the appearance of any variety or novelty of matter and manner. Brainard had too much of the warm spirit of poetry about him, to fall into that artificial mannerism, by which some would impart effect to their ungenial effusions.

Brainard has recommended himself to his countrymen, as a truly *American* poet. His topics, his imgery, his illustrations are mostly of native growth. There is a raciness about them which cannot be mistaken. The reader on this side of the water is familiar with the scenes, the associations, or the incidents to which he is introduced. Most of the common-place of poetry is avoided. The mountains, lakes, rivers, trees, animals, — the characters, pursuits, pastimes, and superstitions, which are touched by the pen of the bard, are American. A foreign reviewer has expressed the opinion, concerning a volume of Selections from American Poets, designed especially to convey strong impressions of the characteristics of the New World, that it conveys no such impression at all, — that, with slight exceptions, one is surprised to find it so truly English, — that its beauties and defects are so similar to the poetry of the parent land. However true this may be in general, yet in regard to Brainard, who is one of the poets from whom selections were made, it cannot be admitted. Scarcely a page is there but shows the American in the topic, the allusion, the scenery, or the characters. He is more truly American, than some English bards are English. Take, for instance, Shenstone, who is, indeed, sufficiently artificial, but whom, however, we mention, because we happened not long since to refresh our memory with his entire poetry. He speaks much of the country and its scenes, particularly in his pastorals and elegies; but it might, in general, as well have been Greece, as Great Britain, — Arcadia as Warwickshire. Fine and sweet as he is, who does not sicken to hear so many changes rung on the pastoral names of Damon, Corydon, Strephon, Phillis, Delia, and Melissa! The kids, the goats, and the lambs of Theocritus and Virgil, figure in the effeminate, though lauded strain. Our native bard has made his mother tongue a better vehicle of American peculiarities, than the Englishman has of the characteristics of Old England. It is, at all events, poetry in which his countrymen can see its reflection of themselves, — their notions, sentiments, usages, and institutions.

Like the great mass of American poetry, Brainard's is *free alike from a vicious and infidel taint*. It is safe to the healthfulness, purity, and peace of the heart to read his productions. A strain of humor, — of merriment may occasionally relax the muscles of the face; but no licentious, and maddening thoughts are suggested by the pictures of his Muse. Generally, a serious, though cheerful and correct view, is taken of human life, and its varied, its vast interests, — of the world and its pursuits, — of the ways of Providence, — and of the truths of Revelation. Occasionally you meet with a sweet religious sentiment, — not perhaps directly and didactically enforced, but incidentally and by allusion, or example, somewhat in the manner of Cowper, in his "Alexander Selkirk."

Brainard's was a short career: had he therefore been characterized by unwonted diligence and energy, he might have failed, by the shortness of life, to realize the highest style of the poetic art. But, inclined as he was, constitutionally, somewhat to the opposite state of mind, and obliged often to write in haste and in other circumstances unfavorable to composition, several of his efforts, as we have already sufficiently admitted, are stamped with a corresponding imperfection. Still, enough has been achieved to rank him as a poet of no ordinary power and maturity. The spirit of song dwelt in him richly, — the success that he met with shows that he did not mistake his vocation, — and it would seem, as if only longer life and additional opportunities were wanting, to the fullest development of poetic excellence.

We subjoin to this sketch, a poetic tribute to the memory of Brainard, from the pen of Snelling. Though it probably expresses, with far too much strength, the poet's trials arising from the deficient patronage and favor of his countrymen at large, it is, in other respects, both just and beautiful.

"PEACE, Muse; a rest thy wearied pinions crave,
Alight, and weep on Brainard's early grave.
Lamented Brainard! Since no living line
Records thy worth, I 'll make that merit mine:
Be mine the task to make fresh roses bloom,
And shed undying fragrance on thy tomb.
In thine own mind our cause of mourning grew, —
The falchion's temper ate the scabbard through.

Hard, hard thy lot, and great thy country's shame,
Who let such offspring die without his fame.
He pined to see the buds his brow that decked,
Nipped by the bitter blight of cold neglect.
Torn from the tree, they perished one by one,
Before their opening petals saw the sun;
While the same chilling blast that breathed on them,
Froze the rich life-blood of the noble stem.
But not neglect, nor sorrow's rankling smart,'
Could sour the kindly current of his heart;
And not the canker that consumed his frame
Could to the last his eagle spirit tame;
With faltering hand his master harp he strung,
While music echoed from his dying tongue,
Then, winged his passage to a higher sphere,
To seek the glory we denied him here.
Fair Cygnus thus, while life's last pulses roll,
Pours forth in melody his parting soul."

MONODY ON THE POET BRAINARD.

By Mrs. L. H. Sigourney.

I roamed where Thames * old Ocean's breast doth cheer,
Pouring from crystal urn, the waters sheen,
What time dim twilight's silent step was near,
And gathering dews impearled the margin green;
Yet, though mild autumn with a smile serene
Had gently fostered summer's lingering bloom,
Methought strange sadness brooded o'er the scene, —
While the lone river, murmuring on in gloom,
Deplored its sweetest bard, laid early in the tomb.

His soul for friendship formed, sublime, sincere, —
Of each ungenerous deed his high disdain,
Perchance the cold world scanned with eye severe; —
Perhaps his harp her guerdon failed to gain; —
But Nature guards his fame, for not in vain
He sang her shady dells, and mountains hoar, —
King Philip's billowy bay repeats his name,
To its gray tower, — and with eternal roar
Niagara bears it on to the far-echoing shore.

Each sylvan haunt he loved, — the simplest flower
That burned Heaven's incense in its bosom fair,
The crested billow with its fitful power, —
The chirping nest, that claimed another's care, —
All woke his worship, as some altar rare
Or sainted shrine doth win the pilgrim's knee; —
And he hath gone to rest, where earth and air
Lavish their sweetest charms, — while loud and free
Sounds forth the wind-swept harp of his own native sea.

* The Thames is a tributary of Long Island Sound, at New London.

His country's brave defenders, few and gray,
By penury stricken, with despairing sighs, —
He nobly sang, and breathed a warning lay
Lest from their graves a withering corse should rise:
But now, where pure and bright, the peaceful skies
And watching stars look down, on Groton's height,
Their monument attracts the traveller's eyes,
Whose souls unshrinking took their martyr-flight,
When Arnold's traitor-sword flashed out in fiendish might.

Youth with glad hand her frolic germs had sown,
And garlands clustered round his manly head, —
Those garlands withered, — and he stood alone
While on his cheek the gnawing hectic fed, —
And chilling death-dews o'er his temple spread: —
But on his soul a quenchless star arose,
Whose hallowed beams their brightest lustre shed
When the dimmed eye to its last pillow goes, —
He followed where it led, and found a saint's repose.

And now, farewell! — The rippling stream shall hear
No more the echo of thy sportive oar;
Nor the loved group, thy father's halls that cheer,
Joy in the magic of thy presence more; —
Long shall their tears thy broken lyre deplore: —
Yet doth thine image, warm and deathless, dwell
With those who love the minstrel's tuneful lore, —
And still thy music, like a treasured spell,
Thrills deep within our souls. Lamented bard, farewell!

TO THE MEMORY OF J. G. C. BRAINARD.

By J. G. Whittier.

Gone to the land of silence, — to the shadows of the dead, —
With the green turf on thy bosom, and the gray stone at thy head!

Hath thy spirit too departed? Doth it never linger here,
When the dew upon the bending flower is falling like a tear?
When the sunshine lights the green earth like the perfect smile of God,
Or when the moonlight gladdens, or the pale stars look abroad?

Hast thou lost thy pleasant fellowship with the beautiful of earth,
With the green trees, and the quiet streams around thy place of birth?
The wave that wanders seaward, — the tall gray hills, whereon
Lingers, as if for sacrifice, the last light of the sun; —
The fair of form, — the pure of soul, — the eyes that shone when thou
Wast answering to their smile of love, — art thou not with them now?

Thou art sleeping calmly, Brainard, — but the fame denied thee when
Thy way was with the multitude, — the living tide of men,
Is burning o'er thy sepulchre, — a holy light and strong,
And gifted ones are kneeling there, to breathe thy words of song, —
The beautiful and pure of soul, — the lights of Earth's cold bowers,
Are twining on thy funeral-stone a coronal of flowers!

Ay, freely hath the tear been given, — and freely hath gone forth
The sigh of grief, that one like thee should pass away from Earth, —
Yet those who mourn thee, mourn thee not like those to whom is given
No soothing hope, no blissful thought, of parted friends in Heaven, —
They feel that thou wast summoned to the Christian's high reward,
The everlasting joy of those whose trust is in the Lord.

FAREWELL TO BRAINARD.

By Deodatus Dutton.

Minstrel, farewell!
Sadly thy harp is slumbering,
Its golden chords unstrung, —
Thy voice, that woke its echoing,
Its cygnet note hath sung;
And voice and harp will slumber on
Till Time's last lingering sands have run:
Minstrel, farewell!

Friend, thou art gone!
We meet no more thy warm embrace,
With cordial friendship stored, —
We greet no more thy welcome face,
Around our social board, —
Thy wonted seat is vacant now,
And thou, our friend, O! where art thou?
Alas! thou 'rt gone!

Brother, adieu!
We mourn thy early destiny,
Thou nearest, dearest, best, —
Ay, bitterly we wept to see,
The grave close o'er thy breast!
But 't was His will; then let us stand
Submissive 'neath his chastening hand!
Brother, adieu!

Son, thou hast fled!
Thou wert a green and verdant leaf,
And *I* am pale and sere!
Yet thou hast fallen! while in grief,
I still am lingering here!
My noble, O! my darling boy,
Thou wert thy father's hope and joy!
Yet thou hast fled.

"Christian, all hail!"
Here with our songs of love and praise,
Thy voice will wake again;
Thy harp in loudest notes shall raise
An everlasting strain!
Our God and thine, who knows no end,
Will be thy Father, Brother, Friend!
"Christian, all hail."

POEMS.

POEMS.

ON CONNECTICUT RIVER.

From that lone lake, the sweetest of the chain
That links the mountain to the mighty main,
Fresh from the rock and swelling by the tree,
Rushing to meet and dare and breast the sea —
Fair, noble, glorious river! in thy wave
The sunniest slopes and sweetest pastures lave;
The mountain torrent, with its wintry roar
Springs from its home and leaps upon thy shore: —
The promontories love thee — and for this
Turn their rough cheeks and stay thee for thy kiss.

Stern, at thy source, thy northern Guardians stand,
Rude rulers of the solitary land,
Wild dwellers by thy cold sequestered springs,
Of earth the feathers and of air the wings;
Their blasts have rocked thy cradle, and in storm
Covered thy couch and swathed in snow thy form —

Yet, blessed by all the elements that sweep
The clouds above, or the unfathomed deep,
The purest breezes scent thy blooming hills,
The gentlest dews drop on thy eddying rills,
By the mossed bank, and by the aged tree,
The silver streamlet smoothest glides to thee.

The young oak greets thee at the water's edge,
Wet by the wave, though anchored in the ledge.
— 'T is there the otter dives, the beaver feeds,
Where pensive oziers dip their willowy weeds,
And there the wild-cat purs amid her brood,
And trains them in the sylvan solitude,
To watch the squirrel's leap, or mark the mink
Paddling the water by the quiet brink; —
Or to out-gaze the gray owl in the dark,
Or hear the young fox practising to bark.

Dark as the frost-nipped leaves that strewed the ground,
The Indian hunter here his shelter found;
Here cut his bow and shaped his arrows true,
Here built his wigwam and his bark canoe,
Speared the quick salmon leaping up the fall,
And slew the deer without the rifle ball,
Here his young squaw her cradling tree would choose,
Singing her chant to hush her swart pappoose,
Here stain her quills and string her trinkets rude,
And weave her warrior's wampum in the wood.

— No more shall they thy welcome waters bless,
No more their forms thy moon-lit banks shall press,
No more be heard, from mountain or from grove,
His whoop of slaughter, or her song of love.

Thou didst not shake, thou didst not shrink when, late
The mountain-top shut down its ponderous gate,
Tumbling its tree-grown ruins to thy side,
An avalanche of acres at a slide.
Nor dost thou stay, when winter's coldest breath
Howls through the woods and sweeps along the heath —
One mighty sigh relieves thy icy breast,
And wakes thee from the calmness of thy rest.

Down sweeps the torrent ice — it may not stay
By rock or bridge, in narrow or in bay —
Swift, swifter to the heaving sea it goes,
And leaves thee dimpling in thy sweet repose.
— Yet as the unharmed swallow skims his way,
And lightly drops his pinions in thy spray,
So the swift sail shall seek thy inland seas,
And swell and whiten in thy purer breeze,
New paddles dip thy waters, and strange oars
Feather thy waves and touch thy noble shores.

Thy *noble* shores! where the tall steeple shines,
At mid-day, higher than thy mountain pines,

Where the white schoolhouse with its daily drill
Of sunburnt children, smiles upon the hill,
Where the neat village grows upon the eye
Decked forth in nature's sweet simplicity —
Where hard-won competence, the farmer's wealth,
Gains merit, honor, and gives labor health,
Where Goldsmith's self might send his exiled band
To find a new "Sweet Auburn" in our land.

What Art can execute, or Taste devise,
Decks thy fair course and gladdens in thine eyes —
As broader sweep the bendings of thy stream,
To meet the southern Sun's more constant beam.
Here cities rise, and sea-washed commerce hails
Thy shores and winds with all her flapping sails,
From Tropic isles, or from the torrid main —
Where grows the grape, or sprouts the sugar-cane —
Or from the haunts, where the striped haddock play,
By each cold northern bank and frozen bay.
Here safe returned from every stormy sea,
Waves the striped flag, the mantle of the free,
— That star-lit flag, by all the breezes curled
Of yon vast deep whose waters grasp the world.

In what Arcadian, what Utopian ground
Are warmer hearts or manlier feelings found,
More hospitable welcome, or more zeal
To make the curious "tarrying" stranger feel

That, next to home, here best may he abide,
To rest and cheer him by the chimney-side ;
Drink the hale Farmer's cider, as he hears
From the gray dame the tales of other years.
Cracking his shag-barks, as the aged crone
— Mixing the true and doubtful into one —
Tells how the Indian scalped the helpless child,
And bore its shrieking mother to the wild,
Butchered the father hastening to his home,
Seeking his cottage — finding but his tomb.
How drums, and flags, and troops were seen on high,
Wheeling and charging in the northern sky,
And that she knew what these wild tokens meant,
When to the Old French War her husband went.
How, by the thunder-blasted tree, was hid
The golden spoils of far famed Robert Kidd;
And then the chubby grandchild wants to know
About the ghosts and witches long ago,
That haunted the old swamp.

The clock strikes ten —
The prayer is said, nor unforgotten then
The stranger in their gates. A decent rule
Of Elders in thy puritanic school.

When the fresh morning wakes him from his dream,
And daylight smiles on rock, and slope, and stream,
Are there not glossy curls and sunny eyes,
As brightly lit and bluer than thy skies ;

Voices as gentle as an echoed call,
And sweeter than the softened waterfall
That smiles and dimples in its whispering spray,
Leaping in sportive innocence away : —
And lovely forms, as graceful and as gay
As wild-brier, budding in an April day ;
— How like the leaves — the fragrant leaves it bears,
Their sinless purposes and simple cares.

Stream of my sleeping Fathers! when the sound
Of coming war echoed thy hills around,
How did thy sons start forth from every glade,
Snatching the musket where they left the spade.
How did their mothers urge them to the fight,
Their sisters tell them to defend the right, —
How bravely did they stand, how nobly fall,
The earth their coffin and the turf their pall.
How did the aged pastor light his eye,
When, to his flock, he read the purpose high
And stern resolve, whate'er the toil may be,
To pledge life, name, fame, all — for Liberty.
— Cold is the hand that penned *that* glorious page —
Still in the grave the body of that sage
Whose lip of eloquence and heart of zeal,
Made Patriots act and listening Statesmen feel —
Brought thy Green Mountains down upon their foes,
And thy white summits melted of their snows,
While every vale to which his voice could come,
Rang with the fife and echoed to the drum.

Bold River! better suited are thy waves
To nurse the laurels clust'ring round their graves,
Than many a distant stream, that soaks the mud
Where thy brave sons have shed their gallant blood,
And felt, beyond all other mortal pain,
They ne'er should see their happy home again.

Thou hadst a poet once, — and he could tell,
Most tunefully, whate'er to thee befell,
Could fill each pastoral reed upon thy shore —
— But we shall hear his classic lays no more!
He loved thee, but he took his aged way,
By Erie's shore, and Perry's glorious day,
To where Detroit looks out amidst the wood,
Remote beside the dreary solitude.

Yet for his brow thy ivy leaf shall spread,
Thy freshest myrtle lift its berried head,
And our gnarled Charter oak put forth a bough,
Whose leaves shall grace thy TRUMBULL'S honored brow.

THE FALL OF NIAGARA.

"Labitur et labetur."

THE thoughts are strange that crowd into my brain,
While I look upward to thee. It would seem
As if GOD poured thee from his "hollow hand,"
And hung his bow upon thine awful front;
And spoke in that loud voice, which seemed to him
Who dwelt in Patmos for his Saviour's sake,
"The sound of many waters"; and had bade
Thy flood to chronicle the ages back,
And notch His cent'ries in the eternal rocks.

Deep calleth unto deep. And what are we,
That hear the question of that voice sublime?
O! what are all the notes that ever rung
From war's vain trumpet, by thy thundering side!
Yea, what is all the riot man can make
In his short life, to thy unceasing roar!
And yet, bold babbler, what art thou to HIM,
Who drowned a world, and heaped the waters far
Above its loftiest mountains? — a light wave,
That breaks, and whispers of its Maker's might.

MATCHIT MOODUS.

A traveller, who accidentally passed through East Haddam made several inquiries as to the "*Moodus noises*," that are peculiar to that part of the country. Many particulars were related to him of their severity and effects, and of the means that had been taken to ascertain their cause, and prevent their recurrence. He was told that the simple and terrified inhabitants, in the early settlement of the town, applied to a book-learned and erudite man *from England*, by the name of Doctor Steele, who undertook, by magic, to allay their terrors; and for this purpose took the sole charge of a blacksmith's shop, in which he worked by night, and from which he excluded all admission, tightly stopping and darkening the place, to prevent any prying curiosity from interfering with his occult operations. He however so far explained the cause of these noises as to say, that they were owing to a carbuncle, which must have grown to a great size, in the bowels of the rocks; and that if it could be removed, the noises would cease, until another should grow in its place. The noises ceased — the doctor departed, and has never been heard of since. It was supposed that he took the carbuncle with him. Thus far was authentic. A little girl, who had anxiously noticed the course of the traveller's inquiries, sung for his further edification the following ballad:

SEE you upon the lonely moor,
A crazy building rise?

No hand dares venture to open the door —
No footstep treads its dangerous floor —
No eye in its secrets pries.

Now why is each crevice stopped so tight?
Say, why the bolted door?
Why glimmers at midnight the forge's light —
All day is the anvil at rest, but at night
The flames of the furnace roar?

Is it to arm the horse's heel,
That the midnight anvil rings?
Is it to mould the ploughshare's steel,
Or is it to guard the wagon's wheel,
That the smith's sledge-hammer swings?

The iron is bent, and the crucible stands
With alchymy boiling up;
Its contents were mixed by unknown hands,
And no mortal fire e'er kindled the brands,
That heated that cornered cup.

O'er Moodus river a light has glanced,
On Moodus hills it shone;
On the granite rocks the rays have danced,
And upward those creeping lights advanced,
Till they met on the highest stone.

O that is the very wizard place,
  And now is the wizard hour,
By the light that was conjured up, to trace
Ere the star that falls can run its race,
  The seat of the earthquake's power.

By that unearthly light, I see
  A figure strange alone —
With magic circlet on his knee,
And decked with Satan's symbols, he
  Seeks for the hidden stone.

Now upward goes that gray old man,
  With mattock, bar, and spade —
The summit is gained, and the toil began,
And deep by the rock where the wild lights ran,
  The magic trench is made.

Loud and yet louder was the groan
  That sounded wide and far;
And deep and hollow was the moan,
That rolled around the bedded stone,
  Where the workman plied his bar.

Then upward streamed the brilliant's light,
  It streamed o'er crag and stone: —
Dim looked the stars, and the moon, that night;

But when morning came in her glory bright,
  The man and the jewel were gone.

But woe to the bark in which he flew
  From Moodus' rocky shore ;
Woe to the captain, and woe to the crew,
That ever the breath of life they drew,
  When that dreadful freight they bore.

Where is that crew and vessel now ?
  Tell me their state who can ?
The wild waves dash o'er their sinking bow —
Down, down to the fathomless depths they go,
  To sleep with a sinful man.

The carbuncle lies in the deep, deep sea,
  Beneath the mighty wave ;
But the light shines upward so gloriously,
That the sailor looks pale, and forgets his glee,
  When he crosses the wizard's grave.

"In the course of our desultory reading we have noted several testimonies of authors and travellers relative to singular noises in the mountains, which would seem almost to corroborate the hypothesis of the Matchit Moodus Alchymist. VASCONCELLOS, a Jesuit of some repute, describes similar noises which he heard in Brazil. They resembled the discharge of heavy artillery. In the Terra de Piratumingo the Indians told him that the noise he heard was an explosion of stones;—'and it was so,' said he, 'for after some days the place was found where a rock had burst, and from its entrails, with the report which we had heard like groans, had sent forth a little treasure. This was a sort of nut, about the size of a bull's heart—full of jewelry of different colors, some white—some transparent crystal, others of a fine red and some between red and white, imperfect as it seemed. All these were placed in order like the grains of a pomegranate, within a case or shell harder than iron, which was broken to pieces by the explosion.' In speaking of the adjoining province of Guayra, TECHO says it is famous for a sort of stones, which nature after a wonderful manner produces in an oval stone case, about the bigness of a man's head:—these stones lying under ground until they arrive to a certain maturity, fly like bombs in pieces about the air, with much noise. In an old account of Teixeira's voyage down the Orellana, the writer says, that 'the Indians assured them, that horrible noises were heard in the Lena de Paraguaxo from time to time, which is a certain sign that this mountain contains stones of great value in its entrails.' HUMBOLDT himself notices this phenomenon as occurring in the hills near Mexico,—a subterraneous noise like the roar of artillery. As coal abounds in those hills, he inquires whether this does not announce a disengagement of hydrogen produced by a bed of coal in a state of inflammation. In the account of the 'Yellow Stone Expedition' of Lewis and Clarke, in 1804, 1805, and 1806, we are told, that, near the falls of the Missouri, several loud reports were heard among the mountains resembling precisely the report of a six-pounder. The Indians had before told them of these noises. The Pawnee and Ricaras tribes of Indians also told the exploring party, that a similar noise was frequently heard among the mountains to the westward of their country, which was caused, they said, by the bursting of the rich mines confined in the bosom of the earth."—J. G. WHITTIER.

ON THE DEATH OF COMMODORE OLIVER H. PERRY.

"By strangers honored, and by strangers mourned."

How sad the note of that funereal drum,
  That 's muffled by indifference to the dead!
And how reluctantly the echoes come,
  On air that sighs not o'er that stranger's bed,
  Who sleeps with death alone.—O'er his young head
His native breezes never more shall sigh;
  On his lone grave the careless step shall tread,
And pestilential vapors soon shall dry
Each shrub that buds around — each flower that blushes nigh.

Let Genius, poising on her full-fledged wing,
  Fill the charmed air with thy deserved praise:
Of war, and blood, and carnage let her sing,
  Of victory and glory! — let her gaze
  On the dark smoke that shrouds the cannon's blaze —

On the red foam that crests the bloody billow ;
Then mourn the sad close of thy shortened days —
Place on thy country's brow the weeping willow,
And plant the laurels thick, around thy last cold pillow.

No sparks of Grecian fire to me belong :
Alike uncouth the poet and the lay ;
Unskilled to turn the mighty tide of song,
He floats along the current as he may,
The humble tribute of a tear to pay.
Another hand may choose another theme,
May sing of Nelson's last and brightest day,
Of Wolfe's unequalled and unrivalled fame,
The wave of Trafalgar — the field of Abraham.

But if the wild winds of thy western lake
Might teach a harp, that fain would mourn the brave,
And sweep those strings the minstrel may not wake,
Or give an echo from some secret cave
That opens on romantic Erie's wave,
The feeble cord would not be swept in vain ;
And though the sound might never reach thy grave,
Yet there are spirits here, that to the strain
Would send a still small voice responsive back again.

And though the yellow plague infest the air ;
Though noxious vapors blight the turf, where rest

The manly form, and the bold heart of war ;
  Yet should that deadly isle afar be blest !
  For the fresh breezes of thy native west
Should seek and sigh around thy early tomb,
  Moist with the tears of those who loved thee best,
Scented with sighs of love — there grief should come,
And mem'ry guard thy grave, and mourn thy hapless doom.

It may not be. Too feeble is the hand,
  Too weak and frail the harp, the lay too brief
To speak the sorrows of a mourning land,
  Weeping in silence for her youthful chief.
Yet may an artless tear proclaim more grief
Than mock affection's arts can ever show ;
  A heart-felt sigh can give a sad relief,
Which all the sobs of counterfeited woe,
Tricked off in foreign garb, can ever hope to know.

A MARINER'S SONG.

Though now we are sluggish and lazy on shore,
Yet soon shall we be where the wild waters roar ;
Where the wind through the hoarse rattling cordage shall rave,
And fling the white foam from the top of the wave.

Yes, soon o'er the waters the Essex shall sweep,
And bear all the thunders of war o'er the deep;
While the hands that are hard, and the hearts that are
brave,
Shall give the bold frigate the top of the wave.

And though some one among us may never return,
His comrades shall sorrow, his messmates shall mourn;
Though his body may sink to a watery gràve,
His spirit shall rise to the top of the wave.

Then a health to John Adams! and long may he reign
O'er the mountain, the valley, the shore, and the main;
May he have the same breeze, which to WASHINGTON
gave,
In his cruise o'er the waters, *the top of the wave.*

EPITHALAMIUM.

I SAW two clouds at morning,
Tinged with the rising sun;
And in the dawn they floated on,
And mingled into one:
I thought that morning cloud was blest,
It moved so sweetly to the west.

I saw two summer currents,
  Flow smoothly to their meeting,
And join their course, with silent force,
  In peace each other greeting :
Calm was their course through banks of green,
While dimpling eddies played between.

Such be your gentle motion,
  Till life's last pulse shall beat;
Like summer's beam, and summer's stream,
  Float on, in joy, to meet
A calmer sea, where storms shall cease —
A purer sky, where all is peace.

INTRODUCTION TO A LADY'S ALBUM.

The wanton boy that sports in May,
Among the wild flowers, blooming, gay,
With laughing eyes and glowing cheeks,
The brightest, freshest, fairest seeks,
And there, delightedly, he lingers,
To pluck them with his rosy fingers,
While, like the bee, he roves among
Their sweets, and hums his little song.

He weaves a garland rich and rare,
And decorates his yellow hair:
The rose, and pink, and violet,
And honeysuckle, there are set;
The darkest cypress in the glade
Lends to the wreath its solemn shade,
And sadly smiles, when lighted up
With daisy, and with butter-cup.

Thus fair and bright each flower should be,
Culled from the field of Poesy;
But with the lightsome and the gay,
Be mixed the moralizing lay
Of those, who, like the cypress bough,
A thoughtful shade of sorrow throw
On transient buds, or flowers light,
That smile at morn, and fade at night.

THE SHAD SPIRIT.

There is a superstition in many places, which bears, that Shad are conducted from the gulf of Mexico into Connecticut river by a kind of *Yankee bogle*, in the shape of a bird, properly called the SHAD SPIRIT. It makes its appearance, annually, about a week before the Shad, calls the fish, and gives warning to the fishermen to mend their nets. It is supposed, that without his assistance, the nets would be swept to no purpose, and the fisherman would labor in vain.

Now drop the bolt, and securely nail
  The horse-shoe over the door;
'T is a wise precaution, and if it should fail
  It never failed before.

Know ye the shepherd that gathers his flock,
  Where the gales of the Equinox blow,
From each unknown reef, and sunken rock,
  In the gulf of Mexico;

While the monsoons growl, and the trade-winds bark,
  And the watch-dogs of the surge
Pursue through the wild waves the ravenous shark,
  That prowls around their charge?

To fair Connecticut's northernmost source,
  O'er sand-bars, rapids, and falls,
The Shad Spirit holds his onward course,
  With the flocks which his whistle calls.

O how shall he know where he went before?
  Will he wander around for ever?
The last year's shad-heads shall shine on the shore,
  To light him up the river.

And well can he tell the very time
  To undertake his task —
When the pork barrel 's low, he sits on the chine,
  And drums on the cider cask.

Though the wind is light, the wave is white,
  With the fleece of the flock that 's near;
Like the breath of the breeze, he comes over the seas,
  And faithfully leads them here.

And now he 's passed the bolted door,
  Where the rusted horse-shoe clings ;
So carry the nets to the nearest shore,
  And take what the Shad Spirit brings.

THE TREE TOAD.

I AM a jolly tree toad, upon a chestnut tree ;
I chirp, because I know that the night was made for me;
The young bat flies above me, the glow-worm shines below,
And the owlet sits to hear me, and half forgets his woe.

I 'm lighted by the fire-fly, in circles wheeling round;
The caty-did is silent, and listens to the sound ;

The jack-o'-lantern leads the way-worn traveller
astray,
To hear the tree toad's melody until the break of day.

The harvest moon hangs over me, and smiles upon
the streams;
The lights dance upward from the north, and cheer
me with their beams;
The dew of heaven, it comes to me as sweet as beau-
ty's tear;
The stars themselves shoot down to see what music
we have here.

The winds around me whisper to ev'ry flower that
blows,
To droop their heads, call in their sweets, and every
leaf to close;
The whip-poor-will sings to his mate the mellow mel-
ody:
"O! hark, and hear the notes that flow from yonder
chestnut tree."

Ye caty-dids and whip-poor-wills, come listen to me
now;
I am a jolly tree toad upon a chestnut bough;
I chirp because I know that the night was made for
me —
And I close my proposition with a Q. E. D.

SPRING.

TO MISS — —.

Other poets may muse on thy beauties, and sing
Of thy birds, and thy flowers, and thy perfumes, sweet
Spring!
They may wander enraptured by hills and by mountains,
Or pensively pore by thy fresh gushing fountains;
Or sleep in the moonlight by favorite streams,
Inspired by the whispering sylphs in their dreams,
And awake from their slumbers to hail the bright sun,
When shining in dew the fresh morning comes on.

But I 've wet shoes and stockings, a cold in my
throat,
The head-ache, and tooth-ache, and quinsy to boot;
No dew from the cups of the flow'rets I sip, —
'T is nothing but *boneset* that moistens my lip;
Not a cress from the spring or the brook can be had:
At morn, noon, and night, I get nothing but shad;
My whispering sylph is a broad-shouldered lass,
And my bright sun — a warming-pan made out o
brass!

Then be *thou* my genius; for what can I do,
When I cannot see *nature*, but copy from *you*?
If Spring be the season of beauty and youth,
Of hope and of loveliness, kindness, and truth;
Of all that 's inspiring, and all that is bright,
And all that is what we call *just about right* —
Why need I expose my sick muse to the weather,
When by going to you she would find all together?

ON THE BIRTHDAY OF WASHINGTON.

"Hic cinis — ubique fama."

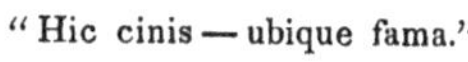

BEHOLD the mossed corner-stone dropped from the wall,
And gaze on its date — but remember its fall,
And hope that some hand may replace it;
Think not of its pride when with pomp it was laid,
But weep for the ruin its absence has made,
And the lapse of the years that efface it.

Mourn WASHINGTON's death, when ye think of his birth,
And far from your thoughts be the lightness of mirth,

And far from your cheek be its smile.
To-day he was born — 't was a loan — not a gift:
The dust of his body is all that is left,
To hallow his funeral pile.

Flow gently, Potomac! thou washest away
The sands where he trod, and the turf where he lay,
When youth brushed his cheek with her wing;
Breathe softly, ye wild winds, that circle around
That dearest, and purest, and holiest ground,
Ever pressed by the footprints of Spring.

Each breeze be a sigh, and each dewdrop a tear,
Each wave be a whispering monitor near,
To remind the sad shore of his story;
And darker, and softer, and sadder the gloom
Of that evergreen mourner, that bends o'er the tomb
Where WASHINGTON sleeps in his glory.

Great GOD! when the spirit of freedom shall fail,
And the sons of the Pilgrims, in sorrow, bewail
Their religion and liberty gone;
O! send back a form that shall stand as *he* stood,
Unsubdued by the tempest, unmoved by the flood;
And to THEE be the glory alone.

LINES SUGGESTED BY A LATE OCCURRENCE.

On the 21st of February, 1823, in the middle of the day, as the mail stage from Hartford to New Haven, with three passengers, was crossing the bridge at the foot of the hill near Durham, the bridge was carried away by the ice, and the stage was precipitated down a chasm of twenty feet. Two of the passengers were drowned: one of them had been long from home, and was on his way to see his friends. This occurrence is mentioned as explanatory of the following lines.

"How slow we drive! — but yet the hour will come,
  When friends shall greet me with affection's kiss;
When, seated at my boyhood's happy home,
  I shall enjoy a mild, contented bliss,
  Not often met with in a world like this!
Then I shall see that brother, youngest born,
  I used to play with in my sportiveness;
And, from a mother's holiest look, shall learn
A parent's thanks to God, for a loved son's return.

"And there is one, who, with a downcast eye
  Will be the last to welcome me; but yet
My memory tells me of a parting sigh,
  And of a lid with tears of sorrow wet,

And how she bade me never to forget
A friend — and blushed. — O! I shall see again
The same kind look I saw, when last we met,
And parted. Tell me *then* that life is vain —
That joy, if met with once, is seldom met again."

* * * * *

* * See ye not the falling, fallen mass?
Hark! hear ye not the drowning swimmer's cry?
Look on the ruins of the desperate pass!
Gaze at the hurried ice that rushes by,
Bearing a freight of woe and agony,
To that last haven where we all must go. —
Resistless as the stormy clouds that fly
Above our reach, is that dark stream below! —
May peace be in its ebb — there 's ruin in its flow.

ON A LATE LOSS.*

> "He shall not float upon his watery bier
> Unwept."

THE breath of air that stirs the harp's soft string,
  Floats on to join the whirlwind and the storm;
The drops of dew exhaled from flowers of spring,
  Rise and assume the tempest's threatening form;
The first mild beam of morning's glorious sun,
  Ere night, is sporting in the lightning's flash;
And the smooth stream, that flows in quiet on,
  Moves but to aid the overwhelming dash
That wave and wind can muster, when the might
  Of earth, and air, and sea, and sky unite.

So science whispered in thy charmed ear,
  And radiant learning beckoned thee away.
The breeze was music to thee, and the clear
  Beam of thy morning promised a bright day.

* Professor FISHER, lost in the Albion, off the coast of Kinsale, Ireland.

And they have wrecked thee! — But there is a shore
  Where storms are hushed — where tempests never
    rage;
Where angry skies and blackening seas, no more
  With gusty strength their roaring warfare wage.
By thee its peaceful margent shall be trod —
  Thy home is Heaven, and thy friend is God.

ON THE DEATH OF REV. LEVI PARSONS.*

Green as Machpelah's honored field,
  Where Jacob and where Leah lie,
Where Sharon's shrubs their roses yield,
  And Carmel's branches wave on high;
So honored, so adorned, so green,
Young martyr! shall thy grave be seen.

O! how unlike the bloody bed,
  Where pride and passion seek to lie;
Where faith is not, where hope can shed
  No tear of holy sympathy!
There withering thoughts shall drop around,
In dampness on the lonely mound.

* He was associated with the Rev. Pliny Fisk, on the Palestine mission, and died at Alexandria, February 18th, 1822.

* * * * *

On Jordan's weeping willow trees,
Another holy harp is hung:
It murmurs in as soft a breeze,
As e'er from Gilead's balm was flung,
When Judah's tears, in Babel's stream
Dropped, and when "Zion was their theme."

So may the harp of Gabriel sound
In the high heaven, to welcome thee,
When, rising from the holy ground
Of Nazareth and Galilee,
The saints of God shall take their flight,
In rapture, to the realms of light.

ON THE PROJECT OF AFRICAN COLONIZATION.

"Magna componere parvis."

All sights are fair to the recovered blind —
All sounds are music to the deaf restored —
The lame, made whole, leaps like the sporting hind;
And the sad, bowed-down sinner, with his load

Of shame and sorrow, when he cuts the cord,
  And drops the pack it bound, is free again
In the light yoke and burden of his Lord :
  Thus, with the birthright of his fellow man,
  Sees, hears, and feels at once, the righted African.

'T is somewhat like the burst from death to life —
  From the grave's cerements to the robes of Heaven ;
From sin's dominion, and from passion's strife,
  To the pure freedom of a soul forgiven !
  When all the bonds of death and hell are riven,
And mortals put on immortality ;
  When fear, and care, and grief away are driven,
And Mercy's hand has turned the golden key,
And Mercy's voice has said, " Rejoice — thy soul is
free ! "

TO THE MARQUIS LA FAYETTE.

We 'll search the earth, and search the sea,
To cull a gallant wreath for thee ;
And every field for freedom fought,
And every mountain height, where aught
Of liberty can yet be found,
Shall be our blooming harvest ground.

aurels in garlands hang upon
Thermopylæ and Marathon —
On Bannockburn the thistle grows —
On Runny Mead the wild rose blows ;
And on the banks of Boyne, its leaves
Green Erin's shamrock wildly weaves.
In France, in sunny France, we 'll get
The fleur-de-lys and mignonette,
From every consecrated spot
Where lies a martyred Huguenot ;
And cull, even here, from many a field,
  And many a rocky height,
Bays that our vales and mountains yield,
  Where men have met, to fight
For law, and liberty, and life,
And died in freedom's holy strife.

Below Atlantic seas — below
  The waves of Erie and Champlain,
The sea-grass and the corals grow
  In rostral trophies round the slain ;
And we can add, to form thy crown,
Some branches worthy *thy* renown !
Long may the chaplet flourish bright,
And borrow from the Heavens its light.
As with a cloud, that circles round
  A star, when other stars have set,
With glory shall thy brow be bound ;

With glory shall thy head be crowned;
  With glory, starlike, cinctured yet!
For earth, and air, and sky, and sea,
Shall yield a glorious wreath to thee.

MANIAC'S SONG.

I can but smile when others weep,
  I can but weep when others smile;
O! let me in this bosom keep
  The secret of my heart awhile.

My form was fair, my step was light,
  As ever tripped the dance along;
My cheek was smooth, my eye was bright —
  My thought was wild, my heart was young.

And he I loved would laugh with glee,
  And every heart but mine was glad;
He had a smile for all but me;
  O! he was gay, and I was sad!

Now, I have lost my blooming health,
  And joy, and hope, no more abide;
And wildering fancies come by stealth,
  Like moonlight on a shifting tide.

They say he wept, when he was told
  That I was sad and sorrowful;
That on my wrist the chain was cold —
  That at my heart the blood was dull.

They fear I 'm crazed — they need not fear,
  For smiles are false, and tears are true;
I better love to see a tear,
  Than all the smiles I ever knew.

TO THE MEMORY OF CHARLES BROCKDEN BROWN.

We seek not mossy bank, or whispering stream,
  Or pensive shade, in twilight softness decked,
Or dewy canopy of flowers, or beam
  Of autumn's sun, by various foliage checked.

Our sweetest river, and our loveliest glen,
  Our softest waterfalls, just heard afar,
Our sunniest slope, or greenest hillock, when
  It takes its last look at the evening star,

May suit some softer soul. But thou wert fit
  To tread our mighty mountains, and to mark,

FACSIMILE OF THE HANDWRITING OF BRAINARD.

Some western muse, if western muse there be,
When the rough wind in clouds has swathed her form
Shall boldly wind her wintry horn for thee
And tune her gusty music to the storm.

The cavern's echoes and the forest's voice
Shall wake in concord to the wailing tone
And winds & waters with their rushing noise
For thee shall make a melancholy moan.

From poem "To the memory of C.B.Brown." p. 37.

In untracked woods, the eagle's pinions flit
O'er roaring cataracts and chasms dark:

To talk and walk with *Nature*, in her wild
Attire, her boldest form, her sternest mood;
To be her own enthusiastic child,
And seek her in her awful solitude.

There, when through stormy clouds, the struggling moon
On some wolf-haunted rock, shone cold and clear,
Thou couldst commune, inspired by *her* alone,
With all her works of wonder and of fear.

Now thou art gone, and who thy walks among,
Shall rove, and meditate, and muse on thee?
No whining rhymster with his schoolboy song,
May wake thee with his muling minstrelsy!

Some western muse, if western muse there be,
When the rough wind in clouds has swathed her form,
Shall boldly wind her wintry horn for thee,
And tune her gusty music to the storm.

The cavern's echoes, and the forest's voice,
Shall chime in concord to the waking tone;
And winds and waters, with perpetual noise,
For thee shall make their melancholy moan.

LORD EXMOUTH'S VICTORY AT ALGIERS.
1816.

"Arma virumque cano."

The sun looked bright upon the morning tide:
Light played the breeze along the whispering shore,
And the blue billow arched its head of pride,
As 'gainst the rock its frothy front it bore;
The clear bright dew fled hastily before
The morning's sun, and glittered in his rays;
Aloft the early lark was seen to soar,
And cheerful nature glorified the ways
Of God, and mutely sang her joyous notes of praise.

The freshening breeze, the sporting wave,
Their own impartial greeting gave
To Christian and to Turk;
But both prepared to break the charm
Of peace, with war's confused alarm —
And ready each, for combat warm,
Commenced the bloody work.

For England's might was on the seas,
With red cross flapping in the breeze,
And streamer floating light;
While the pale crescent, soon to set,
Waved high on tower and minaret,
And all the pride of Mahomet
Stood ready for the fight.

Then swelled the noise of battle high;
The warrior's shout, the coward's cry,
Rung round the spacious bay.
Fierce was the strife, and ne'er before
Had old Numidia's rocky shore
Been deafened with such hideous roar,
As on that bloody day.

It seemed as if that earth-born brood,
Which, poets say, once warred on God,
Had risen from the sea;—
As if again they boldly strove
To seize the thunderbolts of Jove,
And o'er Olympian powers to prove
Their own supremacy.

What though the sun has sunk to rest?
What though the clouds of smoke invest
The capes of Matisou?
Still by the flash each sees his foe,

And, dealing round him death and woe,
With shot for shot, and blow for blow,
  Fights — to his country true.

Each twinkling star looked down to see
The pomp of England's chivalry,
  The pride of Briton's crown!
While ancient Ætna raised his head,
Disgorging from his unknown bed
A fire, that round each hero shed
  A halo of renown.

The dying sailor cheered his crew,
While thick around the death-shot flew;
  And glad was he to see
Old England's flag still streaming high, —
Her cannon speaking to the sky,
And telling all the powers on high,
  Of Exmouth's victory!

The crescent wanes — the Turkish might
Is vanquished in the bloody fight,
  The Pirate's race is run; —
Thy shouts are hushed, and all is still
On tower, and battlement, and hill,
No loud command — no answer shrill —
  Algiers! thy day is done!

The slumb'ring tempest swelled its breath,
And sweeping o'er the field of death,
  And o'er the waves of gore,
Above the martial trumpet's tone,
Above the wounded soldier's moan,
Above the dying sailor's groan,
  Raised its terrific roar.

Speed swift, ye gales, and bear along
This burden for the poet's song,
  O'er continent and sea :
Tell to the world that Britain's hand
Chastised the misbelieving band,
And overcame the Paynim land
  In glorious victory.

WRITTEN FOR A LADY'S COMMONPLACE-BOOK.

Ah ! who can imagine what plague and what bothers
He feels, who sits down to write verses for others !
His pen must be mended, his inkstand be ready,
His paper laid square, and his intellects steady ;
And then for a subject — No, that 's not the way,
For genuine poets don't care *what* they say,

But *how* they shall say it. So now for a measure,
That 's suited alike to your taste and my leisure.
For instance, if you were a matron of eighty,
The verse should be dignified, solemn, and weighty;
And luckless the scribbler who had not the tact,
To make every line a sheer matter of fact.
Or if you were a stiff, worn-out spinster, too gouty
To make a good sylph, and too sour for a beauty;
Too old for a flirt, and too young to confess it;
Too good to complain of 't, and too bad to bless it;
The muse should turn out some unblamable sonnet,
And mutter blank verse in her comments upon it:
Demure in her walk, should look down to her shoe,
And pick the dry pathway, for fear of the dew.

But for *you*, she shall trip it, wherever she goes,
As light and fantastic as L'Allegro's toes;
Wade, swim, fly, or scamper, full-fledged and webb-
footed,
Or on Pegasus mounted, well spurred and well booted,
With martingale fanciful, crupper poetic,
Saddle cloth airy, and whip energetic,
Girths woven of rainbows, and hard-twisted flax,
And horse-shoes as bright as the edge of an axe;
How blithe should she amble and prance on the road,
With a pillion behind for — — — ——.

By Helicon's waters she 'll take her sweet course,
And indent the green turf with the hoofs of her horse;

Up blooming Parnassus bound higher and higher,
While the gate-keeping Graces no toll shall require;
And the other eight Muses shall dance in cotillion,
And sing round the sweep of Apollo's pavillion—
While Phœbus himself, standing godlike on dry land,
Shall shine on the belle of the state of R—— I——.

THE LOST PLEIAD.*

TO MY FRIEND G——.

O! HOW calm and how beautiful—look at the night!
The planets are wheeling in pathways of light;
And the lover, or poet, with heart, or with eye,
Sends his gaze with a tear, or his soul with a sigh.

But from Fesole's summit the Tuscan looked forth,
To eastward and westward, to south and to north;
Neither planet nor star could his vision delight,
'Till his own bright Pleiades should rise to his sight.

They rose, and he numbered their glittering train—
They shone bright as he counted them over again;

* It is said by the ancient poets, that there used to be one more star in the constellation of the Pleiades.

But the star of his love, the bright gem of the cluster,
Arose not to lend the Pleiades its lustre.

And thus, when the splendor of *beauty* has blazed,
On light and on loveliness, how have we gazed!
And how sad have we turned from the sight, when we
found
That the fairest and sweetest was "*not on the ground.*"

THE ALLIGATOR.*

THAT steed has lost his rider! I have seen
His snuffing nostril, and his pawing hoof;
His eyeball lighting to the cannon's blaze,
His sharp ear pointed, and each ready nerve,
Obedient to a whisper; — his white mane
Curling with eagerness, as if it bore,
To squadroned foes, the sign of victory,
Where'er his bounding speed could carry it.
But now, with languid step, he creeps along,
Falters, and groans, and dies.

* The United States schooner Alligator was wrecked on her return from the West India station, after the murder, by the pirates, of her commander, Captain ALLYN.

And I have seen
Yon foundering vessel, when with crowding sail,
With smoking bulwarks, and with blazing sides,
Sporting away the foam before her prow,
And heaving down her side to the brave chase,
She seemed to share the glories of the bold!
But now, with flagging canvass, lazily
She moves; and stumbling on the rock, she sinks,
As broken hearted as that faithful steed,
That lost his rider, and laid down, and died.

THE SEA GULL.*

"Ibis et redibis nunquam peribis in bello." — *Oracle.*

I SEEK not the grove where the wood-robins whistle,
Where the light sparrows sport, and the linnets pair;
I seek not the bower where the ring-doves nestle,
For none but the maid and her lover are there.

On the clefts of the wave-washed rock I sit,
When the ocean is roaring and raving nigh;
On the howling tempest I scream and flit,
With the storm in my wing, and the gale in my eye.

* Commodore PORTER's vessel.

And when the bold sailor climbs the mast,
  And sets his canvass gallantly,
Laughing at all his perils past,
  And seeking more on the mighty sea ;

I 'll flit to his vessel, and perch on the truck,
  Or sing in the hardy pilot's ear ;
That her deck shall be like my wave-washed rock,
  And her top like my nest when the storm is near.

Her cordage, the branches that I will grace —
  Her rigging, the grove where I will whistle ;
Her wind-swung hammock, my pairing place,
  Where I by the seaboy's side will nestle.

And when the fight, like the storm, comes on,
  'Mid the warrior's shout and the battle's noise,
I 'll cheer him by the deadly gun,
  'Till he loves the music of its voice.

And if death's dark mist shall his eye bedim,
  And they plunge him beneath the fathomless wave,
A wild note shall sing his requiem,
  And a white wing flap o'er his early grave.

THE CAPTAIN.

A FRAGMENT.*

Solemn he paced upon that schooner's deck,
And muttered of his hardships: — "I have been
Where the wild will of Mississippi's tide
Has dashed me on the sawyer; — I have sailed
In the thick night, along the wave-washed edge
Of ice, in acres, by the pitiless coast
Of Labrador; and I have scraped my keel
O'er coral rocks in Madagascar seas —
And often in my cold and midnight watch,
Have heard the warning voice of the lee-shore
Speaking in breakers! Ay, and I have seen
The whale and sword-fish fight beneath my bows;
And, when they made the deep boil like a pot,
Have swung into its vortex; and I know

* A Bridgeport paper of March, 1823, said: "Arrived, schooner Fame, from Charleston, via New-London. While at anchor in that harbour, during the rain storm on Thursday evening last, the Fame was run foul of by the wreck of the Methodist Meeting-house from Norwich, which was carried away in the late freshet."

To cord my vessel with a sailor's skill,
And brave such dangers with a sailor's heart;
— But never yet upon the stormy wave,
Or where the river mixes with the main,
Or in the chafing anchorage of the bay,
In all my rough experience of harm,
Met I — a Methodist meeting-house!

* * * * *

Cat-head, or beam, or davit has it none,
Starboard nor larboard, gunwale, stem nor stern!
It comes in such a "questionable shape,"
I cannot even *speak* it! Up jib, Josey,
And make for Bridgeport! There, where Stratford
    Point,
Long-Beach, Fairweather Island, and the buoy,
Are safe from such encounters, we 'll *protest!*
And Yankee legends long shall tell the tale,
That once a Charleston schooner was beset,
Riding at anchor, by a Meeting-house.

LEATHER STOCKING.

The following lines refer to the good wishes which Elizabeth, in MR. COOPER'S novel of "The Pioneers," seems to have manifested, in the last chapter, for the welfare of "Leather Stocking," when he signified, at the grave of the Indian, his determination to quit the settlements of men for the unexplored forests of the west; and when, whistling to his dogs, with his rifle on his shoulder, and his pack on his back, he left the village of Templeton.

FAR away from the hill side, the lake, and the hamlet,
The rock, and the brook, and yon meadow so gay;
From the footpath that winds by the side of the streamlet;
From his hut, and the grave of his friend, far away —
He is gone where the footsteps of men never ventured,
Where the glooms of the wild-tangled forest are centered,
Where no beam of the sun or the sweet moon has entered,
No bloodhound has roused up the deer with his bay.

He has left the green ally for paths, where the bison
Roams through the praries, or leaps o'er the flood;

Where the snake in the swamp sucks its deadliest
 poison,
 And the cat of the mountains keeps watch for its
 food ;
But the leaf shall be greener, the sky shall be purer,
The eye shall be clearer, the rifle be surer,
And stronger the arm of the fearless endurer,
 That trusts nought but Heaven in his way through
 the wood.

Light be the heart of the poor lonely wanderer ;
 Firm be his step through each wearisome mile —
Far from the cruel man, far from the plunderer ;
 Far from the track of the mean and the vile.
And when death, with the last of its terrors, assails him,
And all but the last throb of memory fails him,
He 'll think of the friend, far away, that bewails him,
 And light up the cold touch of death with a smile.

And there shall the dew shed its sweetness and lustre;
 There for his pall shall the oak leaves be spread —
The sweet brier shall bloom, and the wild grape shall
 cluster ;
 And o'er him the leaves of the ivy be shed.
There shall they mix with the fern and the heather ;
There shall the young eagle shed its first feather ;
The wolves, with his wild dogs, shall lie there together,
 And moan o'er the spot where the hunter is laid.

EXTRACTS FROM VERSES WRITTEN FOR THE NEW-YEAR, 1823.

When streams of light, in golden showers,
First fell on long lost Eden's bowers,
And music, from the shouting skies,
Wandered to Eve's own Paradise,
She tuned her eloquent thoughts to song,
And hymned her gratitude among
The waving groves, by goodness planted,
The holy walks by blessings haunted:
And when of bower and grove bereaved,
Since joy was gone, in song she grieved,
And taught her scattering sons the art,
In mirth or woe, to touch the heart.
Bear witness, Jubal's ringing wire,
And untaught David's holier lyre;
Let Judah's timbrel o'er the waters,
Sound to the song of Israel's daughters —
Let Prophecy the strain prolong,
Prompting the watching shepherd's song.
And pressing to her eager lips,
The trump of the Apocalypse.
Bear witness pagan Homer's strain,
That to each valley, hill, and plain

Of classic Greece — to all the isles
That dimple in her climate's smiles —
To all the streams that rush or flow
To the rough Archipelago —
To wood and rock, to brook and river,
Gave names will live in song for ever.

The notes were rude that Druids sung
Their venerable woods among ;
But later bards, enwrapt, could pore
At noon upon their pastoral lore,
And love the oak-crowned shade, that yielded
A blessing on the spot it shielded.
It shed a solemn calm around
Their steps, who trod the Muse's ground;
And waved o'er Shakspeare's summer dreams,
By Avon's fancy-haunted streams.

Then Genius stamped her footprints free,
Along the walks of Poetry ;
And cast a spell upon the spot,
To save it from *the common lot.*
'T was like the oily gloss that 's seen
Upon the shining evergreen,
When desolate in wintry air,
The trees and shrubs around are bare.

And when a New-Year's sun at last
Lights back our thoughts upon the past ;

When recollection brings each loss
Our sad'ning memories across ;
When Piety and Science mourn
PARSONS and FISHER * from them torn —
Just as yon yellow plague has fled —
While mindful mourners wail the dead,
The great, the good, the fair, the brave,
Seized in the cold grasp of the grave ;
When Murder's hand has died the flood
With a young gallant hero's blood;
When cheeks are pale, and hearts distressed,
Is this a time for idle jest?

The waves shall moan, the winds shall wail
Around thy rugged coast, Kinsale,
For one who could mete out the seas,
And turn to music every breeze —
Track the directing star of night,
And point the varying needle right.

Fair Palestine ! is there no sound
That murmurs holy peace around
His distant grave, whose ardent soul
Fainted not till it reached thy goal,

* See note to "Lines on the Death of Rev. Levi Parsons," and "On a late Loss."

And blessed the rugged path, that led
His steps where his Redeemer bled? —
We may not breathe what angels sing —
We may not wake a seraph's string;
Nor brush, with mortal steps, the dew
That heavenly eyes have shed on you.

And who shall tell to listening Glory,
Bending in grief her plumed head,
While war-drops from her brow are shed,
And her beating heart, and pulses numb,
Throb like the tuck of a muffled drum,
Her favorite ALLYN'S* story?
O! other harps shall sing of him,
And other eyes with tears be dim;
And gallant hopes that banish fears,
And hands and hearts, as well as tears,
Shall yet, before *all* eyes are dry,
Do justice to his memory;
And hew or light, with sword or flame,
A pile of vengeance to his name.

O! for those circumscribing seas,
That hemmed thy foes, Themistocles!
When Xerxes saw his vanquished fleet,
And routed army, at his feet —

* See note to "The Alligator."

And scowled o'er Salamis, to see
His foes' triumphant victory!
O! for that more than mortal stand,
Where, marshalling his gallant band,
Leonidas, at freedom's post,
Gave battle to a tyrant's host:
Then Greece might struggle, not in vain,
And breathe in liberty again.

THE NEWPORT TOWER.

When and for what purpose this was built, seems to be matter of dispute. The New-York Statesman associates it with great antiquity — the Commercial Advertiser gives it a military character; and the Rhode-Island American, with a view, perhaps, to save it from doggerel rhymes and sickish paragraphs, says it is nothing but an old windmill — if such was the plan, however, it has not succeeded.

There is a rude old monument,
Half masonry, half ruin, bent
With sagging weight, as if it meant
    To warn one of mischance;
And an old Indian may be seen,
Musing in sadness on the scene,
And casting on it many a keen,
    And many a thoughtful glance.

When lightly sweeps the evening tide
Old Narraganset's shore beside,
And the canoes in safety ride
    Upon the lovely bay —
I 've seen him gaze on that old tower,
At evening's calm and pensive hour,
And when the night began to lour,
    Scarce tear himself away.

Oft at its foot I 've seen him sit,
His willows trim, his walnut split,
And there his seine he loved to knit,
    And there its rope to haul ;
'T is there he loves to be alone,
Gazing at every crumbling stone,
And making many an anxious moan,
    When one is like to fall.

But once he turned with furious look,
While high his clenched hand he shook,
And from his brow his dark eye took
    A red'ning glow of madness ;
Yet when I told him why I came,
His wild and bloodshot eye grew tame,
And bitter thoughts passed o'er its flame,
    That changed its rage to sadness.

"You watch my step, and ask me why
This ruin fills my straining eye?

Stranger, there is a prophecy
    Which you may lightly heed:
Stay its fulfilment, if you can;
I heard it of a gray-haired man,
And thus the threatening story ran, —
    A boding tale indeed.

"*He* said, that when this massy wall
Down to its very base should fall,
And not one stone among it all
    Might rest upon another,
Then should the Indian race and kind
Disperse like the returnless wind,
And no red man be left to find
    One he could call a brother.

"Now yon old tower is falling fast, —
Kindred and friends away are passed;
O! that my father's soul may cast
    Upon my grave its shade,
When some good Christian man shall place
O'er me, the last of all my race,
The last old stone that falls, to grace
    The spot where I am laid."

THE THUNDER STORM.*

THE Sabbath morn came sweetly on,
The sunbeams mildly shone upon
    Each rock, and tree, and flower;
And floating on the southern gale,
The clouds seemed gloriously to sail
Along the Heavens, as if to hail
    That calm and holy hour.

By winding path and alley green,
The lightsome and the young were seen
    To join the gathering throng;
While with slow step and solemn look,
The elders of the village took
Their way, and as with age they shook,
    Went reverently along.

* Two persons, an old lady and a girl, were killed by lightning, in the Presbyterian Meeting-house in Montville, on Sunday the 1st of June, 1823, while the congregation were singing. The following is not an exaggerated account of the particulars.

They meet — the "sweet psalm-tune" they raise ;
They join their grateful hearts, and praise
    The Maker they adore.
They met in holy joy ; but they
Grieve now, who saw *His* wrath that day,
And *sadly* went they all away,
    And *better* than before.

There was one cloud, that overcast
The valley and the hill, nor past
    Like other mists away :
It moved not round the circling sweep
Of the clear sky, but dark and deep,
Came down upon them sheer and steep,
    Where they had met to pray.

One single flash ! it rent the spire,
And pointed downward all its fire —
    What could its power withstay ?
There was an aged head ; and there
Was beauty in its youth, and fair
Floated the young locks of her hair —
    It called them both away !

The Sabbath eve went sweetly down ;
Its parting sunbeams mildly shone
    Upon each rock and flower ;
And gently blew the southern gale,

— But on it was a voice of wail,
And eyes were wet, and cheeks were pale,
In that sad evening hour.

TO A MISSIONARY,

WHO ATTENDED THE LATE MEETING OF THE BIBLE SOCIETY AT NEW YORK.

Why should thy heart grow faint, they cheek be pale?
Why in thine eye should hang the frequent tear,
As if the promise of thy God would fail,
And thou and all be left to doubt and fear?
Doubt not, for holy men are gathered here;
Fear not, for holy thoughts surround the place,
And angel pinions hover round, to bear
To their bright homes the triumphs of His grace,
Whose word all sin and shame, all sorrow shall efface.

Pure as a cherub's wishes be thy thought,
For in thine ear are heavenly whisperings;
And strong thy purposes, as though they sought
To do the errand of the King of Kings.
And if thy heart be right, his mantle flings
Its glorious folds of charity around
Thine earthly feelings; and the tuneful strings

Of harps in heaven shall vibrate to the sound
Of thy soul's prayer from earth, if thou art contrite
found.

Go then, and prosper. He has promised all —
All that instructed zeal can need or ask;
And thou art summoned with too loud a call,
To hesitate and tremble at thy task.
Let scoffers in their glimpse of sunshine bask,
And note thy pilgrimage in *other* light:
Theirs is a look that peeps but through a mask;
Thine is an open path, too plain, too bright
For those who doze by day, and see but in the night.

THE ROBBER.*

THE moon hangs lightly on yon western hill;
And now it gives a parting look, like one

* Two large bags containing newspapers, were stolen from the boot behind a Mail Coach between New Brunswick and Bridgetown. The straps securing the bags in the boot were cut, and nothing else injured or removed therefrom. The letter mails are always carried in the front boot of the coach, under the driver's feet, and therefore cannot be so easily approached.

Who sadly leaves the guilty. You and I
Must watch, when all is dark, and steal along
By these lone trees, and wait for plunder.—Hush!
I hear the coming of some luckless wheel,
Bearing we know not what—perhaps the wealth
Torn from the needy, to be hoarded up
By those who only *count* it; and perhaps
The spendthrift's losses, or the gambler's gains,
The thriving merchant's rich remittances,
Or the small trifle some poor serving girl
Sends to her poorer parents. But come on—
Be cautious.—There—'t is done; and now away,
With breath drawn in, and noiseless step, to seek
The darkness that befits so dark a deed.
Now strike your light.—Ye powers that look upon us!
What have we here? Whigs, Sentinels, Gazettes,
Heralds, and Posts, and Couriers—Mercuries,
Recorders, Advertisers, and Intelligencers—
Advocates and Auroras.—There, what 's that!
That 's—a Price Current.

I do venerate
The man, who rolls the smooth and silky sheet
Upon the well cut copper. I respect
The worthier names of those who *sign* bank bills;
And, though no literary man, I love
To read their short and pithy sentences.
But I hate types, and printers—and the gang

Of editors and scribblers. Their remarks,
Essays, songs, paragraphs, and prophecies,
I utterly detest. — And *these*, particularly,
Are just the meanest and most rascally,
"Stale and unprofitable" publications,
I ever read in my life.

SONNET TO THE SEA-SERPENT.

"Hugest that swims the ocean stream."

WELTER upon the waters, mighty one —
And stretch thee in the ocean's trough of brine;
Turn thy wet scales up to the wind and sun,
And toss the billow from thy flashing fin;
Heave thy deep breathings to the ocean's din,
And bound upon its ridges in thy pride:
Or dive down to its lowest depths, and in
The caverns where its unknown monsters hide,
Measure thy length beneath the gulf-stream's tide —
Or rest thee on that naval of the sea
Where, floating on the Maelstrom, abide
The krakens sheltering under Norway's lee;
But go not to Nahant, lest men should swear,
You are a great deal bigger than you are.

"ĀES ALIENUM."

Hispania! O, Hispania! once my home —
How hath thy fall degraded every son
Who owns thee for a birth-place. They who walk
Thy marbled courts and holy sanctuaries,
Or tread thy olive groves, and pluck the grapes
That cluster there — or dance the saraband
By moonlight, to some Moorish melody —
Or whistle with the Muleteer, along
Thy goat-climbed rocks and awful precipices;
How do the nations scorn them and deride!
And they who wander where a Spanish tongue
Was never heard, and where a Spanish heart
Had never beat before, how poor, how shunned,
Avoided, undervalued, and debased,
Move they among the foreign multitudes!
Once I was bright to the world's eye, and passed
Among the nobles of my native land
In Spain's armorial bearings, decked and stampt
With Royalty's insignia, and I claimed
And took the station of my high descent;
But the cold world has cut a cantle out

From my escutcheon — and now here I am,
A poor, depreciated pistareen.*

THE GUERRILLA.

Though friends are false, and leaders fail,
  And rulers quake with fear;
Though tamed the shepherd in the vale,
  Though slain the mountaineer;
Though Spanish beauty fill their arms,
  And Spanish gold their purse —
Sterner than wealth's or war's alarms,
  Is the wild Guerrilla's curse.

No trumpets range us to the fight;
  No signal sound of drum
Tells to the foe, that in their might
  The hostile squadrons come.
No sunbeam glitters on our spears,
  No warlike tramp of steeds
Gives warning — for the first that hears
  Shall be the first that bleeds.

* This coin, now seldom seen, was formerly valued at twenty cents; but when the above was written passed for but eighteen.

The night breeze calls us from our bed,
At dewfall forms the line,
And darkness gives the signal dread
That makes our ranks combine:
Or should some straggling moonbeam lie
On copse or lurking hedge,
'T would flash but from a Spaniard's eye,
Or from a dagger's edge.

'T is clear in the sweet vale below,
And misty on the hill;
The skies shine mildly on the foe,
But lour upon us still.
This gathering storm shall quickly burst,
And spread its terrors far,
And at its front we 'll be the first,
And with it go to war.

O! the mountain peak shall safe remain —
'T is the vale shall be despoiled,
And the tame hamlets of the plain
With ruin shall run wild;
But Liberty shall breathe our air
Upon the mountain head,
And Freedom's breezes wander here,
Here all their fragrance shed.

JACK FROST AND THE CATY-DID.

JACK FROST.

I HEARD — 't was on an Autumn night —
  A little song from yonder tree;
'T was a Caty-did, in the branches hid,
  And thus sung he:

" Fair Caty sat beside yon stream,
  Beneath the chestnut tree;
Each star sent forth its brightest gleam,
And the moon let fall her softest beam
  On Caty and on me.

" And thus she wished — 'O, could I sing
  Like the little birds in May,
With a satin breast and a silken wing,
And a leafy home by this gentle spring,
  I 'd chirp as blithe as they.

" 'The Frog in the water, the Cricket on land,
  The Night-hawk in the sky,
With the Whip-poor-will should be my band,
While gayly by the streamlet's sand,
  The Lightning-bug should fly.'

"Her wish is granted — Off she flings
  The robes that her beauty hid;
She wraps herself in her silken wings,
And near me now she sits and sings,
  And tells what Caty did."

A beam from the waning moon was shot,
  Where the little minstrel hid,
A cobweb from the cloud was let,
  And down I boldly slid.

A hollow hailstone on my head,
  For a glittering helm was clasped,
And a sharpened spear, like an icicle clear,
  In my cold little fingers was grasped.

Silent, and resting on their arms,
  I viewed my forces nigh,
Waiting the sign on earth to land,
  Or *bivouac* in the sky.

From a birchen bough, which yellow turned
  Beneath my withering lance;
I pointed them to that glassy pool,
  And silently they advanced.

The water crisped beneath their feet
  It never felt their weights;

And nothing but the rising sun,
  Showed traces of their skates.

No horn I sounded, no shout I made,
  But I lifted my vizor lid,
My felt-shod foot on the leaf I put,
  And killed the Caty-did.

Her song went down the southern wind,
  Her last breath up the stream;
But a rustling branch is left behind,
  To fan her wakeless dream.

MR. MERRY'S LAMENT FOR "LONG TOM."*

"Let us think of them that sleep,
  Full many a fathom deep,
  By thy wild and stormy steep,
    Elsinore."

THY cruise is over now,
  Thou art anchored by the shore,
And never more shalt thou
  Hear the storm around thee roar;

* See the sixth chapter of the second volume of "The Pilot," by the author of "The Pioneers."

Death has shaken out the sands of thy glass.
Now around thee sports the whale,
And the porpoise snuffs the gale,
And the night-winds wake their wail,
As they pass.

The sea-grass round thy bier
Shall bend beneath the tide,
Nor tell the breakers near
Where thy manly limbs abide;
But the granite rock thy tombstone shall be.
Though the edges of thy grave
Are the combings of the wave —
Yet unheeded they shall rave
Over thee.

At the piping of all hands,
When the judgment signal's spread —
When the islands, and the lands,
And the seas give up their dead,
And the south and the north shall come;
When the sinner is dismayed,
And the just man is afraid,
Then Heaven be thy aid,
Poor Tom.

ON THE DEATH OF MR. WOODWARD, AT EDINBURGH.

"The spider's most attenuated thread,
Is cord — is cable, to man's tender tie
On earthly bliss; it breaks at every breeze."

ANOTHER! 't is a sad word to the heart,
That one by one has lost its hold on life,
From all it loved or valued, forced to part
In detail. Feeling dies not by the knife
That cuts at once and kills — its tortured strife
Is with distilled affliction, drop by drop
Oozing its bitterness. Our world is rife
With grief and sorrow! all that we would prop,
Or would be propped with, falls — when shall the ruin stop!

The sea has one, and Palestine has one,
And Scotland has the last. The snooded maid
Shall gaze in wonder on the stranger's stone,
And wipe the dust off with her tartan plaid —
And from the lonely tomb where thou art laid,

Turn to some other monument — nor know
  Whose grave she passes, or whose name she read—
Whose loved and honored relics lie below;
Whose is immortal joy, and whose is mortal woe.

There is a world of bliss hereafter — else
  Why are the bad above, the good beneath
The green grass of the grave? The Mower fells
  Flowers and briers alike. But man shall breathe
  (When he his desolating blade shall sheathe
And rest him from his work) in a pure sky,
  Above the smoke of burning worlds; — and Death
On scorched pinions with the dead shall lie,
When time, with all his years and centuries has
  passed by.

TO THE DEAD.

How many now are dead to me
  That live to others yet!
How many are alive to me
Who crumble in their graves, nor see
That sick'ning, sinking look which we
  Till dead can ne'er forget.

Beyond the blue seas, far away,
  Most wretchedly alone,
One died in prison — far away,
Where stone on stone shut out the day,
And never hope, or comfort's ray
  In his lone dungeon shone.

Dead to the world, alive to me;
  Though months and years have passed,
In a lone hour, his sigh to me
Comes like the hum of some wild bee,
And then his form and face I see
  As when I saw him last.

And one with a bright lip, and cheek,
  And eye, is dead to me.
How pale the bloom of his smooth cheek!
His lip was cold — it would not speak;
His heart was dead, for it did not break;
  And his eye, for it did not see.

Then for the living be the tomb,
  And for the dead the smile;
Engrave oblivion on the tomb
Of pulseless life and deadly bloom —
Dim is such glare: but bright the gloom
  Around the funeral pile.

THE DEEP.

There 's beauty in the deep;
The wave is bluer than the sky;
And though the lights shine bright on high,
More softly do the sea-gems glow
That sparkle in the depths below;
The rainbow's tints are only made
When on the waters they are laid,
And Sun and Moon most sweetly shine
Upon the ocean's level brine.
There 's beauty in the deep.

There 's music in the deep: —
It is not in the surf's rough roar,
Nor in the whispering, shelly shore —
They are but earthly sounds, that tell
How little of the sea nymph's shell,
That sends its loud, clear note abroad,
Or winds its softness through the flood,
Echoes through groves with coral gay,
And dies, on spongy banks, away.
There 's music in the deep.

There 's quiet in the deep : —
Above, let tides and tempests rave,
And earth-born whirlwinds wake the wave ;
Above, let care and fear contend,
With sin and sorrow to the end ;
Here, far beneath the tainted foam,
That frets above our peaceful home,
We dream in joy, and wake in love,
Nor know the rage that yells above.
There 's quiet in the deep.

THE GOOD SAMARITAN.

Who bleeds in the desert, faint, naked, and torn,
Left lonely to wait for the coming of morn ?
The last sigh from his breast, the last drop from his heart,
The last tear from his eyelid, seem ready to part.
He looks to the east with a death-swimming eye,
Once more the blest beams of the morning to spy ;
For penniless, friendless, and houseless he 's lying,
And he shudders to think, that in darkness he 's dying.
Yon meteor! — 't is ended as soon as begun —
Yon gleam of the lightning ! it is not the sun ;
They brighten and pass — but the glory of day
Is warm while it shines, and does good on its way.

How brightly the morning breaks out from the east!
Who walks down the path to get tithes for his priest?*
It is not the Robber who plundered and fled;
'T is a Levite. He turns from the wretched his head.
Who walks in his robes from Jerusalem's halls?
Who comes to Samaria from Ilia's walls?
There is pride in his step — there is hate in his eye;
There is scorn on his lip, as he proudly walks by.
'T is thy Priest, thy proud city, now splendid and fair;
A few years shall pass thee, — and who shall be there?

Mount Gerizim looks on the valleys that spread
From the foot of high Ebal, to Esdrelon's head;
The torrent of Kison rolls black through the plain,
And Tabor sends out its fresh floods to that main,
Which, purpled with fishes, flows rich with the dies
That flash from their fins, and shine out from their eyes.†
How sweet are the streams: but how purer the fountain,
That gushes and wells from Samaria's mountain!

---

* Numbers, xviii.

† D'Anville says the fish from which the famous purple die was obtained, were shell-fish; but this is doubted.

From Galilee's city the Cuthite comes out,
And by Jordan-washed Thirza, with purpose devout,
To pay at the altar of Gerizim's shrine,
And offer his incense of oil and of wine.
He follows his heart, that with eagerness longs
For Samaria's anthems, and Syria's songs.

He sees the poor Hebrew: he stops on the way.
— By the side of the wretched 't is better to pray,
Than to visit the holiest temple that stands
In the thrice blessed places of Palestine's lands.
The oil that was meant for Mount Gerizim's ground,
Would better be poured on the sufferer's wound;
For no incense more sweetly, more purely can rise
From the altars of earth to the throne of the skies,
No libation more rich can be offered below,
Than that which is tendered to anguish and woe.

THE NOSEGAY.

I 'LL pull a bunch of buds and flowers,
And tie a ribbon round them,
If you'll but think, in your lonely hours,
Of the sweet little girl that bound them.

I 'll cull the earliest that put forth,
And those that last the longest;
And the bud, that boasts the fairest birth,
Shall cling to the stem that 's strongest.

I 've run about the garden walks,
And searched among the dew, Sir;—
These fragrant flowers, these tender stalks,
I 've plucked them all for you, Sir.

So here 's your bunch of buds and flowers,
And here 's the ribbon round them;
And here, to cheer your saddened hours,
Is the sweet little girl that bound them.

THE STRING AROUND MY FINGER.

"Et hæc olim meminisse juvabit."

THE bell that strikes the warning hour,
Reminds me that I should not linger,
And winds around my heart its power,
Tight as the string around my finger.

A sweet good-night I give, and then
  Far from my thoughts I need must fling her,
Who blessed that lovely evening, when
  She tied the string around my finger.

Lovely and virtuous, kind and fair,
  A sweet-toned bell, O! who shall ring her!
Of her let bell men all beware,
  Who ties such strings around their finger.

What shall I do?—I 'll sit me down,
  And, in my leisure hours, I 'll sing her
Who gave me neither smile nor frown,
  But tied a thread around my finger.

Now may the quiet star-lit hours
  Their gentlest dews and perfumes bring her;
And morning show its sweetest flowers
  To her whose string is round my finger.

And never more may I forget
  The spot where I so long did linger;—
But watch another chance, and get
  Another string around my finger.

SALMON RIVER.*

Hic viridis tenera prætexit arundine ripas
Mincius. — VIRGIL.

'T IS a sweet stream — and so, 't is true, are all
That undisturbed, save by the harmless brawl
Of mimic rapid or slight waterfall,
        Pursue their way
By mossy bank, and darkly waving wood,
By rock, that since the deluge fixed has stood,
Showing to sun and moon their crisping flood
        By night and day.

But yet, there 's something in its humble rank,
Something in its pure wave and sloping bank,
Where the deer sported, and the young fawn drank
        With unscared look;
There 's much in its wild history, that teems
With all that 's superstitious — and that seems
To match our fancy and eke out our dreams,
        In that small brook.

* This river enters into the Connecticut at East Haddam.

Havoc has been upon its peaceful plain,
And blood has dropped there, like the drops of rain;
The corn grows o'er the still graves of the slain —
And many a quiver,
Filled from the reeds that grew on yonder hill,
Has spent itself in carnage. Now 't is still,
And whistling ploughboys oft their runlets fill
From Salmon River.

Here, say old men, the Indian Magi made
Their spells by moonlight; or beneath the shade
That shrouds sequestered rock, or dark'ning glade,
Or tangled dell.
Here Philip came, and Miantonimo,
And asked about their fortunes long ago,
As Saul to Endor, that her witch might show
Old Samuel.

And here the black fox roved, that howled and shook
His thick tail to the hunters, by the brook
Where they pursued their game, and him mistook
For earthly fox;
Thinking to shoot him like a shaggy bear,
And his soft peltry, stripped and dressed, to wear,
Or lay a trap, and from his quiet lair
Transfer him to a box.

Such are the tales they tell. 'T is hard to rhyme
About a little and unnoticed stream,
That few have heard of — but it is a theme
I chance to love;
And one day I may tune my rye-straw reed,
And whistle to the note of many a deed
Done on this river — which, if there be need,
I 'll try to prove.

THE BLACK FOX OF SALMON RIVER.

The lines below are founded on a legend, that is as well authenticated as any superstition of the kind; and as current in the place where it originated, as could be expected of one that possesses so little interest.

"How cold, how beautiful, how bright,
The cloudless heaven above us shines;
But 't is a howling winter's night —
'T would freeze the very forest pines.

"The winds are up, while mortals sleep;
The stars look forth when eyes are shut;
The bolted snow lies drifted deep
Around our poor and lonely hut.

"With silent step and listening ear,
  With bow and arrow, dog, and gun,
We 'll mark his track, for his prowl we hear,
  Now is our time — come on, come on."

O'er many a fence, through many a wood,
  Following the dog's bewildered scent,
In anxious haste and earnest mood,
  The Indian and the white man went.

The gun is cocked, the bow is bent,
  The dog stands with uplifted paw,
And ball and arrow swift are sent,
  Aimed at the prowler's very jaw.

— The ball, to kill that fox, is run
  Not in a mould by mortals made!
The arrow which that fox should shun,
  Was never shaped from earthly reed!

The Indian Druids of the wood
  Know where the fatal arrows grow —
They spring not by the summer flood,
  They pierce not through the winter snow!

Why cowers the dog, whose snuffing nose
  Was never once deceived till now?
And why, amid the chilling snows,
  Does either hunter wipe his brow?

For once they see his fearful den,
'T is a dark cloud that slowly moves
By night around the homes of men,
By day — along the stream it loves.

Again the dog is on his track,
The hunters chase o'er dale and hill,
They may not, though they would, look back,
They must go forward — forward still.

Onward they go, and never turn,
Spending a night that meets no day ;
For them shall never morning sun,
Light them upon their endless way.

The hut is desolate, and there
The famished dog alone returns ;
On the cold steps he makes his lair,
By the shut door he lays his bones.

Now the tired sportsman leans his gun
Against the ruins of the site,
And ponders on the hunting done
By the lost wanderers of the night.

And there the little country girls
Will stop to whisper, and listen, and look,
And tell, while dressing their sunny curls,
Of the Black Fox of Salmon Brook.

ONE THAT 'S ON THE SEA.

WITH gallant sail and streamer gay,
Sweeping along the splendid bay,
That, thronged by thousands, seems to greet
The bearer of a precious freight,
The Cadmus comes; and every wave
Is glad the welcomed prow to lave.
  What are the ship and freight to me —
  I look for one that 's on the sea.

"Welcome FAYETTE," the million cries;
From heart to heart the ardor flies,
And drum, and bell, and cannon noise,
In concord with a nation's voice,
Is pealing through a grateful land,
And all go with him. — Here I stand,
  Musing on one that 's dear to me,
  Yet sailing on the dangerous sea.

Be thy days happy here, FAYETTE —
Long may they be so — long — but yet
To me there 's one that, dearest still,
Clings to my heart and chains my will.

His languid limbs and feverish head
Are laid upon a sea-sick bed.
    Perhaps his thoughts are fixed on me,
    While tossed upon the mighty sea.

I am alone. Let thousands throng
The noisy, crowded streets along:
Sweet be the beam of Beauty's gaze —
Loud be the shout that Freemen raise —
Let Patriots grasp thy noble hand,
And welcome thee to Freedom's land; —
    Alas! I think of none but he
    Who sails across the foaming sea.

So, when the moon is shedding light
Upon the stars, and all is bright
And beautiful; when every eye
Looks upwards to the glorious sky;
How have I turned my silent gaze
To catch one little taper's blaze: —
    'T was from a spot too dear to me,
    The home of him that 's on the sea.

PRESIDENTIAL COTILLION.

Carmina tum melius, cum venerit IPSE canemus.
VIRG. Bucolica, Ecl. ix.

CASTLE GARDEN was splendid one night—though the wet
Put off for some evenings the ball for FAYETTE.
The arrangements were rich, the occasion was pat,
And the whole was in style; — but I sing not of that.

Ye Graces, attend to a poet's condition,
And bring your right heels to the second position;
I sing of a dance, such as never was seen
On fairy-tripped meadow, or muse-haunted green.

The length of the room, and the height of the hall,
The price of the tickets, the cost of the ball,
And the sums due for dresses, I 'm glad to forget —
I 'd rather pay off the whole national debt.

The fiddlers were Editors, ranged on the spot,
There were strings that were rosined, and strings that were not;

Who furnished the instruments I do not know,
But each of the band drew a *very long bow.*

They screwed up their pegs, and they shouldered their
fiddles;
They fingered the notes of their hey-diddle-diddles;
Spectators looked on — they were many a million,
To see the performers in this great cotillion.

One Adams first led Miss Diplomacy out,
And Crawford Miss Money — an heiress no doubt;
And Jackson Miss Dangerous, a tragical actor,
And Clay, Madam Tariff, of home manufacture.

There was room for a set just below, and each buck
Had a belle by his side, like a drake with his duck;
But the first set attracted the whole room's attention,
For they cut the capers most worthy of mention.

They bowed and they courtesied, round went all eight,
Right foot was the word, and *chassé* was the gait;
Then they balanced to partners, and turned them about,
And each one, alternate, was in and was out.

Some kicked and some floundered, some set and some
bounded,
'Till the music was drowned — the figure confounded;
Some danced *dos a dos*, and some danced *contreface*,
And some promenaded — and all lost their place.

In the midst of this great pantomimic *ballette*,
What guest should arrive but the great LA FAYETTE!
The dancers all bowed, and the fiddlers changed tune,
Like Apollo's banjo to the man in the moon.

How sweet were the notes, and how bold was the strain!
O, when shall we list to such concord again?
The hall was sky-covered with Freedom's bright arch,
And it rung to the music of Liberty's march.

SCIRE FACIAS.*

THE BAR *versus* THE DOCKET.

There were but sixty-nine new entries on the docket of the Hartford County Court, at a late session. One of the most important causes is reported below.

THIS action was brought to get cash from the pocket
Of a debtor absconding and absent, called Docket —
For damage sustained by the Bar, through the *laches*†
Of him by whose means the said Bar cut their dashes.

* Make him to know. † Neglect.

They copied the constable, thinking that he
Might have goods in his hands, and be made *Garni-
shee ;* *
Who, being thus summoned to show cause, appeared
To state to the court why he should not be sheared.†

Whereas, said the Plaintiffs, you owe us our living
By *assumpsit implied*, and the costs you must give in —
You have cheated us out of our bread and our butter,
Et alia enormia,‡ too numerous to utter.

Thus solemnly spoke the Bar's counsel, and sighed —
The Garnishee plainly and frankly replied,
That he had no effects, and could not get enough
To pay his own debt, which he thought rather tough.

Then came pleas and rejoinders, rebutters, demurrers,
Such as Chitty would plough into Richard Roe's fur-
rows ; —
Cross questions, and *very* cross answers, to suit —
So the *gist* of the case was the point in dispute. §

---

* One who, being supposed to have in his hands the property of an absconded debtor, is cited to show whether he has or not.

† Not a law *term*, but rather a termination in law.

‡ And other enormities.

§ This is usually the fact before the County Court, and indeed before all other Courts.

The Judges looked grave, as indeed well they might,
For one party was wrong, and the other not right;
The sweeper himself thought it cruel to sue
A man, just because he had nothing to do.

The Docket *non ested*,* the Garnishee proved
That the chattels were gone, and the assets removed—
That they had not been heard of for full half a year,
So he took to the Statute, and swore himself clear.

The case being simple in *English*, the Bench
Resorted, of course, to their old Norman French;
But the Bar being frightened, thought best to defer it,
And pray out the writ *latitat et discurrit.*†

Then a motion was made by the learned debators,
That the sheriff should call out the whole *comitatus*—‡
Read the act—tell the *posse, instanter* to hook it,
And send the whole hue and cry after the Docket.

---

* Not to be found. † Lurks and wanders.
‡ *Posse comitatus*—power of the County.

JERUSALEM.

The following intelligence from Constantinople was of the 11th October, 1824. — "A severe earthquake is said to have taken place at Jerusalem, which has destroyed great part of that city, shaken down the Mosque of Omar, and reduced the Holy Sepulchre to ruins from top to bottom."

FOUR lamps were burning o'er two mighty graves —
Godfrey's and Baldwin's — Salem's Christian kings;
And holy light glanced from Helena's naves,
Fed with the incense which the Pilgrim brings, —
While through the pannelled roof the cedar flings
Its sainted arms o'er choir, and roof, and dome,
And every porphyry-pillared cloister rings
To every kneeler there its "welcome home,"
As every lip breathes out, "O Lord, thy kingdom come."

A mosque was garnished with its crescent moons,
And a clear voice called Mussulmans to prayer.
There were the splendors of Judea's thrones —
There were the trophies which its conquerors wear—
All but the truth, the holy truth, was there: —

For there, with lip profane, the crier stood,
And him from the tall minaret you might hear,
Singing to all whose steps had thither trod,
That verse misunderstood, "There is no God but God."

Hark! did the Pilgrim tremble as he kneeled?
And did the turbaned Turk his sins confess?
Those mighty hands the elements that wield,
That mighty power that knows to curse or bless,
Is over all; and in whatever dress
His suppliants crowd around him, He can see
Their heart, in city or in wilderness,
And probe its core, and make its blindness flee,
Owning Him very God, the only Deity.

There was an earthquake once that rent thy fane,
Proud Julian; when (against the prophecy
Of Him who lived, and died, and rose again,
"That one stone on another should not lie,")
Thou wouldst rebuild that Jewish masonry
To mock the eternal word. — The earth below
Gushed out in fire; and from the brazen sky,
And from the boiling seas such wrath did flow,
As saw not Shinar's plain, nor Babel's overthrow.

Another earthquake comes. Dome, roof, and wall
Tremble; and headlong to the grassy bank,
And in the muddied stream the fragments fall,
While the rent chasm spread its jaws, and drank

At one huge draught, the sediment, which sank
In Salem's drained goblet. Mighty power!
Thou whom we all should worship, praise, and thank,
Where was thy mercy in that awful hour,
When hell moved from beneath, and thine own heaven did lower?

Say, Pilate's palaces — proud Herod's towers —
Say, gate of Bethlehem, did your arches quake?
Thy pool, Bethesda, was it filled with showers?
Calm Gihon, did the jar thy waters wake?
Tomb of thee, *Mary — Virgin* — did it shake?
Glowed thy bought field, Aceldama, with blood?
Where were the shudderings Calvary might make?
Did sainted Mount Moriah send a flood,
To wash away the spot where once a God had stood?

Lost Salem of the Jews — great sepulchre
Of all profane and of all holy things —
Where Jew, and Turk, and Gentile yet concur
To make thee what thou art! thy history brings
Thoughts mixed of joy and woe. The whole earth rings
With the sad truth which He has prophesied,
Who would have sheltered with his holy wings
Thee and thy children. You his power defied:
You scourged him while he lived, and mocked him as he died!

There is a star in the untroubled sky,
That caught the first light which its Maker made —
It led the hymn of other orbs on high ; —
'T will shine when all the fires of heaven shall fade.
Pilgrims at Salem's porch, be that your aid!
For it has kept its watch on Palestine!
Look to its holy light, nor be dismayed,
Though broken is each consecrated shrine,
Though crushed and ruined all — which men have called divine.

NOTE. — Godfrey and Baldwin were the first Christian Kings at Jerusalem. The Empress Helena, mother of Constantine the Great, built the *church of the sepulchre* on Mount Calvary. The walls are of stone and the roof of cedar. The four lamps which light it are very costly. It is kept in repair by the offerings of Pilgrims who resort to it. The Mosque was originally a Jewish Temple. The Emperor Julian undertook to rebuild the temple of Jerusalem at very great expense, to disprove the prophecy of our Saviour, as it was understood by the Jews; but the work and the workmen were destroyed by an earthquake. The pools of Bethesda and Gihon — the tomb of the Virgin Mary, and of King Jehoshaphat — the pillar of Absalom — the tomb of Zachariah — and the *campo santo*, or holy field, which is supposed to have been purchased with the price of Judas's treason, are, or were lately, the most interesting parts of Jerusalem.

ISAIAH, CHAPTER XXXV.

A ROSE shall bloom in the lonely place,
  A wild shall echo with sounds of joy,
For heaven's own gladness its bounds shall grace,
  And forms angelic their songs employ.

And Lebanon's cedars shall rustle their boughs,
  And fan their leaves in the scented air;
And Carmel and Sharon shall pay their vows,
  And shout, for the glory of God is there.

O, say to the fearful, be strong of heart,
  He comes in vengeance, but not for thee;
For thee He comes, his might to impart
  To the trembling hand and the feeble knee.

The blind shall see, the deaf shall hear,
  The dumb shall raise their notes for Him,
The lame shall leap like the unharmed deer,
  And the thirsty shall drink of the holy stream.

And the parched ground shall become a pool,
  And the thirsty land a dew-washed mead,

And where the wildest beasts held rule,
The harmless of His fold shall feed.

There is a way, and a holy way,
Where the unclean foot shall never tread,
But from it the lowly shall not stray,
To it the penitent shall be led.

No lion shall rouse him from his lair,
Nor wild beast raven in foaming rage;
But the redeemed of the earth shall there
Pursue their peaceful pilgrimage.

The ransomed of God shall return to him
With a chorus of joy to an angel's lay;
With a tear of grief shall no eye be dim,
For sorrow and sighing shall flee away.

THE INDIAN SUMMER.

WHAT is there sadd'ning in the Autumn leaves?
Have they that "green and yellow melancholy"
That the sweet poet spake of? — Had he seen
Our variegated woods, when first the frost

Turns into beauty all October's charms—
When the dread fever quits us — when the storms
Of the wild Equinox, with all its wet,
Has left the land, as the first deluge left it,
With a bright bow of many colors hung
Upon the forest tops — he had not sighed.

The moon stays longest for the Hunter now:
The trees cast down their fruitage, and the blithe
And busy squirrel hoards his winter store:
While man enjoys the breeze that sweeps along
The bright blue sky above him, and that bends
Magnificently all the forest's pride,
Or whispers through the evergreens, and asks,
"What is there sadd'ning in the Autumn leaves?"

WRITTEN FOR AN ALBUM.

SEE to your book, young lady; let it be
An index to your life — each page be pure,
By vanity uncolored, and by vice
Unspotted. Cheerful be each modest leaf,
Not rude; and pious be each written page,
Without hypocrisy, be it devout;

Without moroseness, be it serious ;
If sportive, innocent: and if a tear
Blot its white margin, let it drop for those
Whose wickedness needs pity more than hate.
Hate *no one* — hate their *vices*, not themselves.
Spare many leaves for charity — that flower
That better than the rose's first white bud
Becomes a woman's bosom. There we seek
And there we find it first. Such be your book,
And such, young lady, always may you be.

ON THE LOSS OF A PIOUS FRIEND.

Imitated from the 57th chapter of Isaiah.

Who shall weep when the righteous die ?
  Who shall mourn when the good depart ?
When the soul of the godly away shall fly,
  Who shall lay the loss to heart ?

He has gone into peace — he has laid him down
  To sleep till the dawn of a brighter day ;
And he shall wake on that holy morn,
  When sorrow and sighing shall flee away.

But ye who worship in sin and shame
  Your idol gods, whate'er they be ;
Who scoff in your pride at your Maker's name,
  By the pebbly stream and the shady tree —

Hope in your mountains, and hope in your streams,
  Bow down in their worship and loudly pray;
Trust in your strength and believe in your dreams,
  But the wind shall carry them all away.

There 's one who drank at a purer fountain,
  One who was washed in a purer flood:
He shall inherit a holier mountain,
  He shall worship a holier God.

But the sinner shall utterly fail and die —
  Whelmed in the waves of a troubled sea ;
And God from his throne of light on high
  Shall say, there is no peace for thee.

THE TWO COMETS.

There were two visible at the time this was written; and for the verses, they were, on other accounts, strictly *occasional.*

THERE once dwelt in Olympus some notable oddities,
For their wild singularities called Gods and Goddesses. —
But one in particular beat 'em all hollow,
Whose name, style, and title was Phœbus Apollo.

Now Phœb. was a genius — his hand he could turn
To any thing, every thing genius can learn:
Bright, sensible, graceful, *cute*, spirited, *handy*,
Well bred, well behaved — a celestial Dandy!
An eloquent god, though he did n't *say* much;
But he drew a long bow, spoke Greek, Latin, and Dutch;
A doctor, a poet, a soarer, a diver,
And of horses in harness an excellent driver.

He would tackle his steeds to the wheels of the sun,
And he drove up the east every morning, *but one;*

When young Phaeton begged of his daddy at five,
To stay with Aurora a day, and *he'd* drive.
So good-natured Phœbus gave Phaey the seat,
With his mittens, change, waybill, and stage-horn complete;
To the breeze of the morning he shook his bright locks,
Blew the lamps of the night out, and mounted the box.
The *crack* of his whip, like the *breaking* of day,
Warmed the wax in the ears of the leaders, and they
With a snort, like the fog of the morning, cleared out
For the west, as young Phaey meant to get there about
Two hours before sunset.

He looked at his "*turnip*,"
And to make the delay of the old line concern up,
He gave 'em the reins; and from Aries to Cancer,
The style of his drive on the road seemed to answer;
But at Leo, the ears of the near-wheel horse pricked,
And at Virgo the heels of the off leader kicked;
Over Libra the whiffle-tree broke in the middle,
And the traces snapped short, like the strings of a fiddle.
One wheel struck near Scorpio, who gave it a roll,
And set it to buzz, like a top, round the pole;
While the other whizzed back with its linchpin and hub,
Or, more learnedly speaking, its nucleus or nub;

And, whether in earnest, or whether in fun,
He carried away a few locks of the sun.

The state of poor Phaeton's coach was a blue one,
And Jupiter ordered Apollo a new one;
But our driver felt rather too proud to say "Whoa,"
Letting horses, and harness, and every thing go
At their terrified pleasure abroad; and the muse
Says, they cut to this day just what capers they choose;
That the eyes of the chargers as meteors shine forth;
That their manes stream along in the lights of the north;
That the wheels which are missing are comets, that run
As fast as they did when they carried the sun;
And still pushing forward, though never arriving,
Think the west is before them, and Phaeton driving.

TO A YOUNG FRIEND LEARNING TO PLAY THE FLUTE.

There 's a wild harp, which unconfined by rule
Of science, varies with the varying air,
And sympathizes with the free-born wind;
Swelling, whene'er the tempest swells, or sad

When the soft western-breeze in moans goes down,
And sighs, and dies away. 'T is sweet to mark
Its tone, and listen in some musing mood
To its strange cadence. Be your music such,
And let it die at sundown if you please.

EXTRACTS FROM NEW-YEAR'S VERSES FOR 1825.

I LOVE the "Universal Yankee Nation,"
  Where'er they are — whate'er they are about,
Whatever be their wealth, or rank, or station,
  Their character or conduct. They are out
Upon parole, or suff'rance, or probation,
  On horse-back, or on foot — and some, no doubt,
In coaches, or in Congress! — bless the land,
It is a thing I cannot understand.

By Yankee, I mean every man that 's born
  Within a tract of country, bounded East
By the Atlantic — South, (not by Cape Horn)
  But by Long Island Sound, and on the West
By New York State; northward by the forlorn
  Hope of the British, (a poor rhyme at best)
Mountains and rocks and rivers far away,
That see six months of night, and six of day.

These Yankees are a scattered race — each breeze
That sweeps a prairie, or that wakes a wave,
Is their acquaintance ; forests, lakes, and seas
Know them — adventurous, cunning, tough, and brave,
Shrewd and inquisitive ; they know their P's
And Q's. They know to earn, and get, and save ;
And if they break a thing, why, they can mend it :—
Their cash they get abroad, and then come home to spend it.

Plymouth and Bunker Hill are Yankee places,
And them I 'll celebrate with pen and ink ;
They are the themes of glory — and the traces
Of blood and prayer are on their brow and brink ;
And every reverential thought which graces
The Yankee heart, that will but stop and think
Of what those fathers were, is like the tear
Which children shed upon a parent's bier.

That silent, moonlight march to Bunker Hill,
With spades, and swords, bold hearts, and ready hands,
That Spartan step without their flutes — that still,
Hushed, solemn music of the heart, commands
More than the trumpet's echo — 't is the thrill
That thoughts of well-loved homes, and streams, and lands,

Awaken when men go into the fight,
As did the men at Bunker Hill that night.

And blessed be that ever-coming wave,
  That wets the rock where the old Pilgrims landed;
Thrice blessed be that foothold of the brave,
  Where Freedom stood, and Tyranny was stranded;
Where Persecution, baffled, found its grave,
  And naked Liberty — there — single handed,
Met foe and famine, pestilence and wrath,
And stayed till nought was left to cross her path.

Such themes are far too eloquent for me,
  And few or none can do them justice; yet
'T would be a proud day in one's life to see
  The look of Webster — or to hear Fayette
Give his last blessing to *that* Hill, and be
  Near the brave spot with Warren's life-blood wet —
— That glorious *lachrymal of patriot's tears* —
And boast of such a sight in after years.

THE DOG-WATCH.

On the homeward passage, in the merchant service, the mate keeps the watch from six to eight. This is called the Dog-Watch.

SWEEP on, the wave is curled with foam,
Sweep on, the tide is bearing home,
Sweep on, the breeze is fair;
The sun himself hastes to the West,
Where lies the home that I love best, —
Wave, tide, and breeze may rage or rest
When I get there.

The twilight smiles upon the sea,
The stars shine out to pilot me;
And one, amidst the glare
Of all their host, — the *evening star*
Stoops sweetly o'er my home afar,
And says no storm my course shall mar,
Till I get there.

The list'ning of an anxious ear,
The gaze that brightens through a tear,
Out-feel the watcher's round.

I only hear the breakers roar,
I only see my own dear shore,
'T is *I* that soon shall tread once more
My native ground.

SONNET.

TO A LADY ON THE DEATH OF MRS. — — —.

Weep, if you have a tear to spare,
For her who once like you was fair;
Who led like you the dance and song,
And tripped bright fashion's paths along —
Who in maturer years looked round
With circumspective eye — that found
Beneath the circuit of the sun
Nought it could safely rest upon.

That eye looked upward, far away,
And gazed upon another day.
Closed its pure lid on all below —
Sin, folly, vanity, and woe:
On Death's black wing her willing flight
Rose into uncreated light.

SKETCH OF AN OCCURRENCE ON BOARD A BRIG.

I.

THE sun's beam and the moon's beam check the sea,
The light wave smiles in both, and sportingly
Catching the silver on its deep blue side,
Throws it in spangles on the westering tide,
And tints the golden edges of the beam
That last and sweetest trembles on the stream;
For sure 't is moonlight — see the sun give way,
And yon fair orb light up another day,
A calmer, softer morning than the hour
Of real morn, howe'er bedecked with flower,
Or bud, or song, or dew-drop — the sun's feast,
Or all the gorgeous glories of the East.

What boat is that! yon lonely little boat,
Sculling and rippling through the shades, that float
On yon sequestered bay; and mark the trees,
Bending so beautifully in the breeze.
It steals from out the shade, and now the tide
Presses its bow and chafes against its side;

She seems to wear her way with little strength,
Feeble, but yet determined, till at length
The skiff comes near and nearer — "boat ahoy!
What scull is that, and who are you, my boy?"

II.

There is a tear in that young, sullen eye,
That looks not like a boy's tear, soon to dry;
There is a tremor on his lip and chin,
A mixed up look — half feeling and half sin.
Panting with toil or anger, now he stands
Upon the deck, and wrings his blistered hands,
Too proud to weep, — too young to wear the face
Of manhood steeled to danger, pain, disgrace;
There was in lip, and cheek, and brow, and eye,
A gesture of each thought's variety,
While leaning sadly 'gainst the vessel's wale,
He told, in broken words, a common tale.
He was a runaway, — had left the shore,
Stolen a boat, a jacket, and an oar,
And come on board our brig, "in hopes that we,"
(He said,) "would take him with us out to sea."
The captain hushed at once the poor boy's fears:
— We want a cabin boy — dry up your tears;
The wind calls for us, spread the loftiest sail,
And catch the top-most favor of the gale;
The tide sets out, the ocean 's on the lea,
Gayly we 'll plough our furrow through the sea.

III.

The eye, the ear, the nostril, and the heart,
How they do snuff and listen, gaze, and start,
When the brave vessel strains each brace and line,
Mounts the mad wave, and, dashing through its brine,
Flies from the thick'ning anger of the spray,
And doubly swift leaps forward on her way ;
While the keen seaman takes his watchful stand,
And feels the tiller tremble in his hand —
Or lashed securely on the sea-washed side,
Heaves lead, or log, and sings how fast they glide.

But that young boy: I think I see him now,
With death upon his eye-lid and his brow ;
That eye so blue and clear, that forehead fair,
Those ringlets, too, of close-curled, glossy hair,
That hectic flush, which to the last grew bright,
As his next world's young dawning grew more light ; —
Yes ! that young boy — the danger and the pain
Of hardships past — the thought that ne'er again
His foot might press the paths his boyhood loved,
Or his hand lift the latchet unreproved,
His ear hear sweet forgiveness — or his eye
See those he loved even from his infancy, —
And then the giddy whirl of his young brain,
Upon the rushing, changing, tumbling main,
Without a friend to look at, by his side,
He wept, and said his prayers, and groaned, and died.

IV.

They plunged him, when the winds were up, and when
The sharks played round this floating home of men;
When the strained timbers groaned in every wave,
And the rough cordage screamed above his grave;
When the wild winds wove many a sailor's shroud
Of darkness in the red-edged thunder cloud;
While in the dread black pauses of the storm,
The stunned ear heard his moan, the shut eye saw his
form.
Had it been calm — had dolphins played in rings,
And flying fishes sunned their wetted wings;
Had the sweet south but breathed to smooth the sea,
And evening, for one hour, looked tranquilly;
Or had some tomb-like iceberg floated on
The spot, as the retiring sun went down,
Or the black Peteril on mid-ocean's surge
Sung to the Albatross the poor boy's dirge, —
One might have blest the far off, long lost spot
Where to the deepest depths he sunk and was forgot.
Silent they bore him to the vessel's side,
Silent the hammock and the rope they eyed,
With thoughtful look, a moment there they stood,
And gazed an instant on the yawning flood;
A sailor's prayer, a sailor's tear, were all
They had to give him, but a sailor's pall —
They plunged him in the water, and the shark
Plunged after him, down, down, into the dark.

V.

On rolls the storm — once more the sky is blue,
And there is mirth among the hardy crew ;
The port is gained, the vessel waits the breeze,
To bear her once again o'er tides and seas
Back to her home : our native hills once more
Send the land breezes from the well-known shore,
And, as the joys and pains of memory come,
The questioned pilot tells us news of home.

Once more upon the land! — What sweet-eyed girl
With long bright locks, clustered in many a curl
Round her white polished forehead, sits alone
In anxious sadness on yon wave washed stone !
Her eye looks searchingly from face to face,
One long sought look or lineament to trace ;
In vain the ear grates to each loud rough cry
Of boisterous welcome, or of coarse reply, —
In vain that hand is stretched his hand to grasp,
In vain those arms his well loved form to clasp ;
A few shrill piercing words — 't was all she said —
" O tell me, is my brother " —— " he is dead." —

As the struck bird will rise upon the wing,
And whirl aloft in agonizing swing,
Then seek the darkest covert of the wood,
To pant, and bleed, and die in solitude —

That fair form flitted to the forest shade,
Where sank, and died alone, the broken-hearted maid.

STANZAS.

The dead leaves strew the forest walk,
  And withered are the pale wild flowers ;
The frost hangs black'ning on the stalk,
  The dewdrops fall in frozen showers.
  Gone are the Spring's green sprouting bowers,
Gone Summer's rich and mantling vines,
  And Autumn, with her yellow hours,
On hill and plain no longer shines.

I learned a clear and wild-toned note,
  That rose and swelled from yonder tree —
A gay bird, with too sweet a throat,
  There perched and raised her song for me.
  The winter comes, and where is she ?
Away — where summer wings will rove,
  Where buds are fresh, and every tree
  Is vocal with the notes of love.

Too mild the breath of southern sky,
  Too fresh the flower that blushes there,

The northern breeze that rustles by,
  Finds leaves too green, and buds too fair;
  No forest tree stands stripped and bare,
No stream beneath the ice is dead,
  No mountain top with sleety hair
Bends o'er the snows its reverend head.

Go there, with all the birds, — and seek
  A happier clime, with livelier flight,
Kiss, with the sun, the evening's cheek,
  And leave me lonely with the night.
  — I 'll gaze upon the cold north light,
And mark where all its glories shone —
  See — that it all is fair and bright,
Feel — that it all is cold and gone.

REVERY.

Yes, there are thoughts that have no sound — such thoughts
That no coined phrase of words can utter them!
The tongue would syllable their shapes in vain —
The cautious pen, even in a master's hand,
Finds nothing at its point to mark them with.

No earthly note can touch these airy chords;
'T is silent music — indescribable.
We hear it when the ear is shut, and see
Its beauties when the eye is closed in sleep;
We feel it when the nerves are all at rest —
When the heart stops, and the charmed soul throbs on.
The immaterial pulses of that soul
Will revel to its harmonies, as if
Even in this mortal life 't were "fancy free"
From the gross business of the body's care.

These are not of our make — they come sometimes,
When the sad sleeper has forgot his woes,
And given his agonies awhile to rest.
Through the still watches of the solemn night,
They pace with fairy feet the labyrinths
Of the brain's thousand cares, and lightly sweep
Its pains away for many a star-lit hour —
— But then the morning comes, and where are they?
Perhaps they visit to console the good —
Perchance to hurry on to his dark fate
The bad, and strew with flowers his way to death.

NEW YEAR'S VERSES.

FOR THE CARRIER OF THE MIRROR. 1826.

THE carrier is a poor old man —
See his gray locks, his wrinkles scan,
  Look at him and admire!
His coat is thin, his jacket torn,
All but his fob and pockets worn —
  Such is his poor attire.

And what the scorching sun could throw —
And what the winter's pelting snow
  Could give him, he has stood.
There is one earthly torment lacking —
One other process — that of hacking: —
  He has not been reviewed.

Now for our annual New Year's song.
Short was the year, and not too long
  Shall be the rhymer's strain:
It tells of all that all well know,
'T is mixed of folly and of woe —
  Of happiness, and pain.

How like the seasons was the year!
Now rough, and rude — now mild, and clear,
  Like March, and June together:
Now sweeping on with fury's blast —
Now stilly breathing on the past,
  And calming all its weather.

When streams were stiff and snow was deep —
When Statesmen's promises were cheap,
  And honesty near frozen;
When votes were counted, State by State,
Mid friends and foes — mid joy and hate,
  A President was chosen.

Curst was the siroc, steaming hot,
When patriot against patriot
  Was set in mad array;
And doubly curst that poisoned trail,
That lingers, when the sweeping gale
  Has moaned and died away.

Our tree was fair in trunk and shoot,
Its verdant boughs bore flower and fruit
  That ripened in the sun;
Why should the bramble shoot its thorn,
When of the fruits these stems had borne
  The hand could pluck but one.

* * * * *

Fayette! the skies were bright to thee,
And our small State right proud may be
  That on thy stormy track,
Her sons were guides; for she may boast,
That ALLEN brought thee to our coast,
  And MORRIS bore thee back.

How did the blessed rainbow shed
Its gorgeous colors on your head,
  When first you saw the shore:
How did it arch above your sail,
And span the bay, and tinge the gale,
  And dye the waters o'er.

The Cadmus saw its tinted line,—
It smiled upon the Brandywine;
  And how it shone on high,
He who can paint a rainbow's hues,
And dip his pencil in its dews,
  May better tell than I.

Warm be your hearth, and full your store
And open as your hand, your door;—
  And gently on your heart
Fall every blessing Heaven can shed,
Upon the virtuous patriot's head,
  Till soul and body part.

* * * * *

I hear a sorrowing western breeze,
Sigh from Champlain's dark ice-girt seas —
  Yet 't is a wind-harp strain ; —
It mourns so sweetly, that its tone
Has consolation in its moan,
  And soothing in its pain.

Brave Downie ! thou had'st often seen
The bold in combat, and had'st been
  Where decks and waves were gore ;
Thy gallant foe, thy noble friend,
Has met in peace a Christian's end, —
  Macdonough is no more.

He sleeps in quiet, by the side
Of wife and children dear ; — nor pride
  Nor pomp his tomb adorning :
The clods, the dust, his body cover,
But round him shall the angels hover,
  " Till the bright morning."

* * * * *

On Groton heights, the lazy cow
Is grazing round the grass-grown brow
  That once, in days gone by,
Was rough with pike and bayonet,
Stained with the carnage red and wet,
  Of brave men met to die.

They died. — And must their memories die ?
O ! the weeper's sob and the mourner's sigh
Are quickly, quickly gone.
To the devotion of that band,
That cutlass drew and rampart manned,
That fought their foeman hand to hand,
That saved the honor of your land,
And died where their intrenchments stand,
Ye will not raise a stone.

But be it so. Whate'er the cause,
They fought not thus for vain applause —
'T was patriot duty pressed them ;
And in their rough and gory shroud,
Without the purple of the proud,
God in his mercy rest them.

Yet shall those graves, unknown so long
To memory's tear and glory's song,
Be ever blest.
Green, rank, and bright the turf shall grow
Above the mouldered bones below —
" Rest, warriors, rest."

* * * * *

Now sullenly the damp winds blow,
And muddily the waters flow,

And fast the rain-drops fall;
Such is the time to hope that soon
A heaven-bright sun, a cloudless moon,
Shall shine upon us all.

The time is up, the morrow's dawn
Breaks on a purer, holier morn
Than Pagan new-year's day;
It comes not out in mirth and song,
It calls the vain world's passing throng,
To meet, and praise, and pray.

How should this hour, between the day
When God to Israel's array
Proclaimed the holy rest —
And that which saw a Saviour rise,
With our redemption to the skies —
How should such hour be blessed.

TO A DEAF AND DUMB LADY.

I WISH — 't is no concern of mine,
But yet I wish that you would try
The painter's brush, and trace the line
Of grace or beauty by the eye; —

And teach the hand the tongue's strange art
To tell the stories of the heart.

For you have never heard a sound,—
  Have never uttered with the tongue
The music of your looks, nor found
  A voice their sweetness to prolong.
Shall such soul in such body dwell,
A pearl within a pearly shell?

Try! words are colors;—Feeling lays
  Their tints on memory's open page,
Now bright, now soft, now dim their rays,
  They gleam in youth and fade in age.
Yet when their hues are gone, each stain
That daubed their beauties will remain.

A purer pallet grace your hand,
  A purer pencil follow on,
(Obedient to the eye's command,)
  The objects that you think upon.
For you, from half our frailties free,
Might paint a page of purity.

I 've seen what I would you could see,
  The calm, the breeze, the gale, the motion
Of elements combined—yet free,
  Each for itself, to vex the ocean;

And thought that words would ill supply
The cravings of the straining eye.

I 've seen what you have seen, the sky
  As pure as innocence could make it,
As blue and bright as beauty's eye,
  With not a tearful wink to shake it.
Ask not for words in such an hour,
Nor the ear's listening — listening power.

Sense is not competent to tell
  The strivings of the clay-bound soul;
Thoughts high as heaven and deep as hell,
  Will awfully around it roll;
And words are sacrilege, that dare
Its fearful workings to declare.

AN EVENING CLOUD.

Yon cloud, 't is bright and beautiful — it floats
Alone in God's horizon — on its edge
The stars seem hung like pearls — it looks as pure
As 't were an angel's shroud — the white cymar
Of Purity just peeping through its folds,
To give a pitying look on this sad world.

Go visit it, and find that all is false;
Its glories are but fog — and its white form
Is plighted to some thunder-gust. —
The rain, the wind, the lightning have their source
In such bright meetings. Gaze not on the clouds,
However beautiful — Gaze at the sky —
The clear, blue, tranquil, fixed, and glorious sky.

ON THE DEATH OF ALEXANDER,

EMPEROR OF THE RUSSIAS, AT TAGANROK.

Napoleon died upon Helena's rock; —
Round and beneath were piled and stored the waves,
Mighty and fathomless. Atlantic's shock
Recoiled, and through its deepest, coldest caves,
Of pillared spar and coral architraves,
Did ocean's homage to that strange man's death.
Bad was he, but yet great. Of kings, of slaves,
Of popes, the equal dread. His latest breath
Fell where the waters washed to shore his sea-green wreath.

But thou, by Asian Azof's shallow pool,
Where the Don pours its tributary mud,
Where nought but cold Cimmerian blasts have rule,
And Kalmuck's hungry Tartars fight for food;

Thou, whom we once thought wise, and great, and
good —
Peace, such as thou did'st wish to all, abide
With thee — a despot's peace. So let the flood
Of memory stagnate round thee, like the tide
That washes Taganrok from Azof's shallowest side.

Then let the Cossack trail his barb'rous lance,
And learn to do the obsequies of Czars;
Teach his wild horse around thy grave to prance,
And know the sounds of amens from hurras.
He, paid in plunder for his wounds and scars,
Rejoices that another chance may come,
When southward, in the strife of Turkish wars,
That horse shall hear Tambourgi's muffled drum,
And trample, not as now, on many a lordly tomb.

* * * * *

Fair Liberty! Nor he of Helen's Isle,
Nor he of Azof's side, were born of thee;
Children of cruelty, long nursed by guile,
They claim no tear of tribute from the free.
Then let the despots rest. But where is he
Who, pure in life, majestic in his fall,
Lay down beneath his native cedar-tree?
Potomac's wave, Mount Vernon's grassy pall,
That wraps his relics round, O! these are worth
them all.

SNOW IN APRIL.

"My head is gray, but not with years."

An April snow! — 't is as the head of youth
Just fresh'ning in the spring-time of its hopes,
And glancing to the sunbeam the bright eye,
And to the first rose pouting its rich lip,
Or turning to the morning's blush its cheek,
And to the morning's music its young ear —
Dimpling its chin, as April's rain-drops fall
On the brook's eddy, — 't is as if such head
Of smile, and bloom, and dimple, were adorned
With the white locks of age, that venerably
Spread monitorial sadness — premature;
Weaving the bleached and silvery threads of time,
On the bright texture of a glad boy's eyelash.

So move we on. I 've seen the eye of age
Bright to the last as that of Moses was, —
I 've marked the foot-falls of a man, whose years
Were more than eighty — firm and active too.

Who has not seen the young lid close in pain,
The young knee tremble, and the young heart sink,
And age, old age, encourage and support,
Even as the tree stands, when the buds are nipped,
Tenacious 'till they *would* fall off, — and then
Bearing the loss!—I've wandered from the theme —
Why should I not? "My heart is in the coffin,"
Long shall I "pause till it come back to me."

TO A LADY WHO HAD LOST A RELATIVE.

No more to grace the happy hearth,
  To grace the cheerful board, no more
To light with smiles the misty path
  That leads to the eternal shore,
  Arrived — embarked, and all is o'er.
The sunny curl, the bright blue eye,
  The form, the soul are gone before,
And we must follow on, and die.

And she, the aged one, bereaved,
  Sits lonely in a daughter's chair,
Submissive to God's will, yet grieved,
  Raising to Heaven the silent prayer;
  Her faith and love and hopes are there —

But where are yours? and where are mine?
The prospect, is it bright or drear?
The comfort, human or divine?

THE MOCKING-BIRD.

It has a strange wild note — that Mocking-bird,
I 've heard him whistle to the passer by,
And scold like any parrot. Now his note
Mounts to the play-ground of the lark — high up,
Quite to the sky. And then again it falls,
As a lost star falls, down into the marsh,
The veriest puddle — but it stops not thus;
'T will croak like any bull-frog, or 't will squeal
Like an old rat, caught tight in the toothed spring
Of man's humane contrivancy — and then
Rejoicing, mock the trap, and yell out "*cheese.*"
So mock we all, and so we imitate
The good a little, and the bad a deal.
The notes of heaven, of earth, sometimes of hell
Are on our tongue-tips. Hear the little wretch,
How he does sing, and scream, and mock us all.

THE SWEETBRIER.

Our sweet autumnal western-scented wind
  Robs of its odors none so sweet a flower,
In all the blooming waste it left behind,
  As that the sweetbrier yields it. And the shower
  Wets not a rose that buds in beauty's bower
One half so lovely, —yet it grows along
  The poor girl's pathway — by the poor man's door.
Such are the simple folks it dwells among:
And humble as the bud, so humble be the song.

I love it, for it takes its untouched stand
  Not in the vase that sculptors decorate, —
Its sweetness all is of my native land,
  And e'en its fragrant leaf has not its mate
  Among the perfumes which the rich and great
Buy from the odors of the spicy east.
  You love *your* flowers and plants — and will you hate
The little four-leaved rose that I love best,
That freshest will awake, and sweetest go to rest?

SONG—IF I COULD LOVE.

If I could love, I 'd find me out
  A roguish, laughing eye,
A cheek to blush, a lip to pout,
  A pure, kind heart, to sigh.

A fairy hand, to touch and glance,
  From note to note with glee,
A fairy foot to trip the dance
  And lead it down with me.

A soul to share in all my fun,
  And feel for all my woes,
And as our little life should run
  To take it as it goes.

And O, when follies all have fled
  And solemn thoughts shall rise,
To soothe me on my dying bed
  And meet me in the skies.

Such thoughts are vain, too vain — yet why
Should you such thoughts reprove —
O pity, pity me, for I
Am poor, and cannot love.

QUI TRANSTULIT SUSTINET.*

The warrior may twine round his temples the leaves
Of the Laurel that Victory throws him;
The Lover may smile as he joyously weaves
The Myrtle that beauty bestows him.
The Poet may gather his ivy, and gaze
On its evergreen honors enchanted;
But what are their ivys, their myrtles, and bays,
To the vine that our forefathers planted.

Let France boast the lily — let Britain be vain
Of her thistles, and shamrocks, and roses;
Our shrubs and our blossoms sprout out from the main,
And our bold shore their beauty discloses.
With a home and a country, a soul and a God,
What freeman with terrors is haunted,
Bedecked with the dewdrops and washed with the flood
Is the vine that our forefathers planted.

* Motto of the Arms of Connecticut.

Then a health to the brave, and the worthy, that bore
  The vine whose rich clusters o'ershade us;
They planted its root by the rocks of the shore,
  And called down His blessing who made us.
—And a health to the Fair who will raise up a brave
  Generation of Yankees undaunted,
To nourish, to cherish, to honor, and save
  The vine that our forefathers planted.

DIRGE.

ON THE DEATH OF ADAMS AND JEFFERSON.*

Toll not the bell, and muffle not
The drum, nor fire the funeral shot;
Nor half way hoist our banner now—
Nor weed the arm, nor cloud the brow,—
But high to heaven be raised the eye,
And holy be the rapturous sigh:
And still be cannon, drum, and bell,
Nor let the flag of sorrow tell.

Now low are laid their honored forms,
But from the clods, and dust, and worms,

* Attempted to the tune of "Roslin Castle."

Their spirits wake, and, breathing, rise
Above the sun's own glorious skies.
And happy be their airy track —
We may not, would not, call them back; —
For patriot hands may clasp with theirs,
And Angel harps may hymn their prayers.

TO A LADY FOR A NOSEGAY.

— "*Plenis manibus, ferte lilia, ferte.*"

Who does not love a flower?
Its hues are taken from the light,
Which summer's sun flings pure and bright,
In scattered and prismatic hues,
That shine and smile in dropping dews;
Its fragrance from the sweetest air,
Its form from all that 's light and fair; —
Who does not love a flower?

A lesson to the giver.
Not in the streets to bloom and shine,
Not in the rout of noise and wine,
Not trampled by the rushing crowd,

Not in paved streets and cities proud—
From danger safe, from blighting tree,
Pure, simple, artless, let it be
An emblem of the giver.

"STIFLED WITH SWEETS."

Was I not served in open day
With buds and flowers!—and whence came they?
In the still night, as poets tell,
Queen Mab rings out her little bell,
And sends her sylphs on moonlight beams,
To weave our happy, youthful dreams,
(—Ere morning crimsons for the day
That comes to chase them all away—)
To whisper in the slumberer's ear,
Thoughts full of young and buoyant cheer;
To put such nectar to the lip
As waking mortals never sip—
To place a rosebud on each eye,
To purify the sleeper's sigh,
And best of all, beside his couch
Leave on his cheek a Fairy's touch.
But who, in honest open day,
Sends buds and flowers—and whence come they?

A RAINY DAY.

It rains. What lady loves a rainy day?
Not she who puts prunella on her foot,
Zephyrs around her neck, and silken socks
Upon a graceful ancle — nor yet she
Who sports her tasselled parasol along
The walks, beau-crowded on some sunny noon,
Or trips in muslin, in a winter's night
On a cold sleigh-ride — to a distant ball.
She loves a rainy day who sweeps the hearth,
And threads the busy needle, or applies
The scissors to the torn or threadbare sleeve;
Who blesses God that she has friends and home;
Who, in the pelting of the storm, will think
Of some poor neighbour that she can befriend;
Who trims the lamp at night and reads aloud,
To a young brother, tales he loves to hear;
Or ventures cheerfully abroad, to watch
The bedside of some sick and suffering friend, —
Administering that best of medicine,
Kindness, and tender care, and cheering hope;
— Such are not sad, e'en on a rainy day.

SONNET.

TO —— ——.

—♦—

— SHE was a lovely one — her shape was light
And delicately flexible ; her eye
Might have been black, or blue, — but it was bright,
Though beaming not on *every* passer-by ;
'T was very modest, and a little shy.
The eyelash seemed to shade the very cheek ;
That had the color of a sunset sky,
Not rosy — but a soft and heavenly streak
For which the arm might strike — the heart might break —
And a soft gentle voice, that kindly sweet
Accosted one she chanced to overtake,
While walking slowly on iambic feet,
In tones that fell as soft as heaven's own dew —
Who was it ! dear young Lady, was it you ?

TO THE MOON.

"O, thou."—CLAUD HALCRO.

BLESS thy bright face! though often blessed before
By raving maniac and by pensive fool;
One would say something more — but who as yet,
When looking at thee in the deep blue sky,
Could tell the poorest thought that struck his heart?
Yet all have tried, and all have tried in vain.
At thee, poor planet, is the first attempt
That the young rhymster ventures. And the sigh
The boyish lover heaves, is at the Moon.
Bards, who — ere Milton sung or Shakspeare played
The dirge of sorrow, or the song of love,
Bards, who had higher soared than Fesole,
Knew better of the Moon. 'T was there they found
Vain thoughts, lost hopes, and fancy's happy dreams,
And all sweet sounds, such as have fled afar
From waking discords, and from daylight jars.
There Ariosto puts the widow's weeds
When she, new wedded, smiles abroad again,
And there the sad maid's innocence — 't is there

That broken vows and empty promises,
All good intentions, with no answering deed
To anchor them on the substantial earth,
Are shrewdly packed. — And could he think that thou,
So bright, so pure of aspect, so serene,
Art the mere storehouse of our faults and crimes?
I 'd rather think as puling rhymsters think,
Or love-sick maidens fancy — Yea, prefer
The dairy notion that thou art but cheese,
Green cheese — than thus misdoubt thy honest face.

THE GRAVE-YARD.

'T is morning on the sunny sod,
Where lingering footsteps late have trod;
'T is morning on the melting snow,
That shrouds the graves of those below;
'T is morning to each sprouting thing,
That greenly smiles because 't is spring;
'T is morning on the marble stones,
That designate their owners' bones;
'T is morning to the young and fair,
That walk, and laugh, and loiter there
Above let spring in brightness glow,
A brighter morning smiles below.

There is a beam, that breaks upon
The lone forsaken buried one ;
And, clearer than that dawning ray,
Which gives the first sweet light of day,
Sheds on the Christian's soul a light
To which the noonday sun is night ;
And shows the path his Saviour trod,
When, rising, he returned to God.

THE SEA-BIRD'S SONG.

On the deep is the mariner's danger,
On the deep is the mariner's death ;
Who, to fear of the tempest a stranger,
Sees the last bubble burst of his breath ?
'T is the sea-bird, sea-bird, sea-bird,
Lone looker on despair ;
The sea-bird, sea-bird, sea-bird,
The only witness there.

Who watches their course, who so mildly
Careen to the kiss of the breeze ?
Who lists to their shrieks, who so wildly
Are clasped in the arms of the seas ?
'T is the sea-bird, &c.

Who hovers on high o'er the lover,
  And her who has clung to his neck ?
Whose wing is the wing that can cover,
  With its shadow, the foundering wreck ?
    'T is the sea-bird, &c.

My eye in the light of the billow,
  My wing on the wake of the wave ;
I shall take to my breast for a pillow,
  The shroud of the fair and the brave.
    I 'm a sea-bird, &c.

My foot on the iceberg has lighted,
  When hoarse the wild winds veer about ;
My eye, when the bark is benighted,
  Sees the lamp of the Light-House go out.
    I 'm the sea-bird, sea-bird, sea-bird,
      Lone looker on despair ;
    The sea-bird, sea-bird, sea-bird,
      The only witness there.

STANZAS.

On the lake of young life is a fairy boat,
  Like the sweet new moon in a summer sky ;

Through a calm of brightness it seems to float,
And in light and beauty its course to ply.
As sudden as a cricket's spring
Its feathery paddles dip the seas,
As gayly as the hum-bird's wing
Its sails arrest the scented breeze;
And pennons bright and streamers gay
Flutter above the diamond spray,
As the keel cuts its wimpling way.

A little boy — they call him Love —
With dimpled cheek and sunny brow,
And pinions like a nestling dove,
Sits laughing on the fairy prow.
And one as rosy bright as he,
Bearing his torch of purest light,
With more of joy and less of glee,
Trims the gay bark, and shapes aright
The course, as they distance to weather and lee
The scud of the sky, and the foam of the sea.

Two forms are their lading, two hearts are their care,
And precious the charge that they joy to convey;
The young and the happy, the brave and the fair,
Have sped on their journey, how blithely away!
But as the moon, which shone but now
A silver streak of heavenly light,
With added glory on her brow

Now nobly walks the queen of night —
And firmly moves, though clouds arise,
By storm and tempest fiercely driven,
Shrouding the blue and starry skies,
And darkening all the lights of heaven —
Thus sped the boat; each wale became
Of strong and more enduring frame,
And sternly to the sweeping blast
Stood out the tall and gallant mast.

That boy has strength and courage high,
And manhood lights with thought his eye ;
And he, the pilot, sits demure
In dignity, serene, secure.
Yes, all have left their brightness now,
A brighter hope is on each brow ;
No fancied chart, of fairy bays
And elfin isles, direct their ways —
A heavenly guide sits kindly there,
Directing the course of the brave and the fair ;
In yon blessed place be their anchor cast,
And holy the haven they find at last.

HYMN

FOR THE ANNIVERSARY OF THE HARTFORD COUNTY AGRICULTURAL SOCIETY. 1826.

To Thee, O God, the Shepherd Kings
  Their earliest homage paid,
And wafted upon angel wings
  Their worship was conveyed.

And they who "watched their flocks by night,"
  Were first to learn thy grace, —
Were first to seek by dawning light,
  Their Saviour's dwelling-place.

The hills and vales, the woods and streams,
  The fruits and flowers are thine ;
Where'er the sun can send its beams,
  Or the mild moon can shine.

By Thee, the Spring puts forth its leaves,
  By Thee, comes down the rain,
By Thee, the yellow harvest sheaves
  Stand ripening on the plain.

When Winter comes in storm and wrath,
  Thy soothing voice is heard;
As round the Farmer's peaceful hearth
  Is read Thy holy word.

Thus are we fostered by Thy care,
  Supported by Thy hand;
Our heritage is rich and fair,
  And this Thy chosen land.

Be Joseph yet a fruitful vine,*
  Whose branches leap the wall,
Make Thou its clusters ever Thine,
  Jehovah, God of all.

STANZAS.

My hopes were as bright as the bow, when the storm
  Is rolling away before it,
And Love painted on them so bright a form
  That not a cloud came o'er it.

* Genesis xlix. 22.

The bow has gone, and the night come on,
And all is dark and dreary;
Love has departed, and hope has flown
To the silent grave of Mary.

My thoughts were as playful as billows, that kiss
The rocks and the sands of the shore;
And fancy would whisper, like them, of a bliss
Such as mortal ne'er met before.

But the billows are lost in a whelming wave,
Whose voice shall be never weary;
And Fancy has withered, like weeds on the grave
Of my loved, my ruined Mary.

There was joy in her cheek, there was love in her eye,
And innocence played around her;
But her laugh of mirth was changed to a sigh
When the toils of deception bound her.

Now dead is he that beguiled my love,
And she that I loved so dearly;
And I shall join, in the heaven above,
My bright, angelic Mary.

TO A CHILD, THE DAUGHTER OF A FRIEND.

I PRAY thee by thy mother's face,
  And by her look, and by her eye,
By every decent matron grace
That hovered round the resting-place
  Where thy young head did lie;
And by the voice that soothed thine ear,
The hymn, the smile, the sigh, the tear
  That matched thy changeful mood;
By every prayer thy mother taught —
By every blessing that she sought,
  I pray thee to be good.

Is not the nestling, when it wakes
  Its eye upon the wood around,
And on its new fledged pinions takes
Its taste of leaves and boughs and brakes —
  Of motion, sight, and sound —
Is it not like the parent? Then
Be like thy mother, child, and when
  Thy wing is bold and strong,
As pure and steady be thy light —
As high and heavenly be thy flight —
  As holy be thy song.

THE INVALID

ON THE EAST END OF LONG ISLAND.

Feeble, with languid, staff-supported step,
And heavy eye and heavier heart, I tread
The sun-scorched sand, and breathe the sultry air
That hovers on the road. One effort more,
One mile or two at most, and then I stand
Where I can feel the balmy breath of heaven.
The grassy lane, o'er-arched with boughs and leaves,
Runs its green vista to a small bright point,
And that point is the ocean. Faint the limbs,
And all the body tires — but for the soul,
It hath its holyday in such a spot.

A moment rest we on the only stone
In all the alley — wipe the sweating brow,
And drop the eye upon the turf around.

The notes of birds are heard in other groves,
And everywhere are welcome ; for the song
Of gladness and of innocence is sweet
To all. But here and to the weary too

'T is exquisite: for with it comes the sound,
Not of the wind-fanned leaves and rustling boughs,
And wavy tree-tops only — but the voice
Of ocean.

He has heard its mighty sound
Whose bark was on its awful waters, when
The billows swept the deck and rioted,
Mixed with the winds, round all its gallant spars.
He too has heard its moanings, who, becalmed
Lies like a small thing, helpless and alone
Upon a rolling, waste immensity.
And he has heard another tone, who marks
Its furious dance among the leeward rocks,
Where he must bear its ravings o'er his bones.
But in this calm and leafy grove, the sound
Is smoother, softer, sweeter, than the harp
That the winds love to play on. Let us rise
And view the Giant that can tune his voice
To every passion — that can touch each chord
That vibrates in a saint's or sinner's heart.
— But to the shore. O! what a depth of wave,
And what a length of foam! That solemn voice!
'T is louder and yet sweeter — They mistake
Who call it hoarse — They never on the white
And pebbly beach in peace and quietness
Have heard it roar — or watched the spray
That, venturing furthest on the smooth, white sand,
Kisses, retires, and comes to kiss again.

Upon the utmost bound, a clear, white jet
Of water, from the dark green wave, betrays
The sporting of the whale ; and nearer shore
The sea-birds rise upon their wetted wings,
And bear their prey far to their lonely nests.

The sun sets — and the blushing water turns
To a blue, star-spread, foam-tipped, wavy sea
Of beauty. Yonder sweeps a brave white sail,
Bending as gracefully in evening's breeze
As a keen skater on the glassy ice.
And now — even as some hospitable man
Will light his going guest into the path,
And bid God bless him, as he speeds his way
Onward, alone, into the untried dark,
The Lighthouse – last of friends that ship may see,
Points out the course, till far beyond its beam
The sea fire of the ocean only shines.

Away — from all that 's bright, and beautiful ;
From the fresh breeze and from the glorious view,
From all that 's lovely, noble, or sublime,
To the sick pillow and the feverish bed.
There may good angels watch me, and good thoughts
Crowd to my dreaming and my waking hours ;
For the whole world of waters, the firm land,
The canopy, with all its suns and stars,
Its bright, unnumbered systems, all are His,
And He is everywhere.

HOW TO CATCH A BLACK-FISH.

Thomson, the poet of the year, has sung
And melodized the cautious, sylvan art,
To lure the trout from underneath the root
Of some old oak, or tempt him from his rock
Deep-shelving far beneath the grassy bank,
Where all is always shadow — to the stream
That sparkles in the sunbeam. Thence the hook
Drags him in speckled beauty to the shore.

The bard of Scotland and of nature sung
For this, thy praise, sweet Thomson — yea, and he
Of loftier thought, and bolder hand, declared
To nymphs and swains where their own Druid slept.
But who shall sing his praise, who tells the world
The way to catch a black-fish? Praise, 't is said,
Is not a plant of mortal soil — 't is naught —
And naughty is the wish to cull its weeds.

Begin then, Muse, and help me to the bait,
That, when the sea retires, will shelter close
Beneath the sea-weed side of rocks and stones;

And gange,* sweet maid of Hellas — gange my hook
So that, nor steady pull may draw it off,
Nor cumbrous thread betray its fell design, —
Sit on the bow, fair sister to the eight
Who on Parnassus miss thy absence strange,
And let me scull to where the young flood lifts
The rockweed, as the morning breeze wakes up
The daisy that the lark has slept beside.
So wakes the Black-fish, and with lazy fin
Paddles his round white nose in curious search
For meat untoiled for, yet expected much.
Beware! Thy guardian genius with her wings
Of silkiness — her breath of sea-shell air —
Her voice the whispering of the smallest bubble
That rises from the oozy depths around,
All give thee warning, Touch not! — 'T is in vain.
The subtle bait is sought for greedily,
And swallowed without tasting — next he lies
Panting and bleeding by the fisher's side.
And does he pause to moralize? — No, no,
He baits the hook to tempt another on,
And feasts upon their folly.

* A term well known among fishermen; and meaning to knit, or by any other mode unite, the hook with the line.

THE STORM OF WAR.

O! ONCE was felt the storm of war!
It had an earthquake's roar;
It flashed upon the mountain height,
And smoked along the shore.

It thundered in a dreaming ear,
And up the Farmer sprang;
It muttered in a bold, true heart,
And a warrior's harness rang.

It rumbled by a widow's door,—
All but her hope did fail:
It trembled through a leafy grove,
And a maiden's cheek was pale.
It steps upon the sleeping sea,
And waves around it howl;
It strides from top to foaming top,
Out-frowning ocean's scowl.

And yonder sailed the merchant ship—
There was peace upon her deck;
—Her friendly flag from the mast was torn,
And the waters whelmed the wreck.

But the same blast that bore her down
  Filled a gallant daring sail,
That loved the might of the black'ning storm,
  And laughed in the roaring gale.

The stream, that was a torrent once,
  Is rippled to a brook,
The sword is broken, and the spear
  Is but a pruning hook.
The mother chides her truant boy,
  And keeps him well from harm;
While in the grove the happy maid
  Hangs on her lover's arm.

Another breeze is on the sea,
  Another wave is there,
And floats abroad triumphantly,
  A banner bright and fair;
And peaceful hands and happy hearts,
  And gallant spirits keep
Each star that decks it pure and bright,
  Above the rolling deep.

THE MONEY DIGGERS.

It is a fact that two men from Vermont (July 11th, 1827) were working by the side of one of the wharves in New London, for buried money, by the advice and recommendation of an old woman of that State, who assured them, that she could distinctly see a box of dollars packed edge-wise. The locality was pointed out to an inch, and her only way of discovering the treasure was by looking through a stone, which to ordinary optics was hardly translucent. For the story of the Spanish Galleon, that left so much bullion in and about New London, see Trumbull's History of Connecticut, and for Kidd, inquire of the oldest lady you can find.

Thus saith The Book — "Permit no witch to live;"
Hence, Massachusetts hath expelled the race, —
Connecticut, where swap and dicker thrive,
Admits not to their foot a resting-place.
With more of hardihood and less of grace,
Vermont receives the sisters gray and lean,
Allows each witch her airy broomstick race,
O'er mighty rocks and mountains dark with green,
Where tempests wake their voice, and torrents roar between.

And one there was among that wicked crew,
To whom the enemy a pebble gave,
Through which, at long-off distance, she might view
All treasures of the fathomable wave;
And where the Thames' bright billows gently lave,
The grass-grown piles that flank the ruined wharf,
She sent *them* forth, those two adventurers brave,
Where greasy citizens their bev'rage quaff,
Jeering at enterprise — aye ready with a laugh.

They came — those straight-haired, honest meaning
men,
Nor question asked they, nor reply did make,
Albeit their locks were lifted like as when
Young Hamlet saw his father. And the shake
Of knocking knees and jaws that seemed to break,
Told a wild tale of undertaking bold,
While as the oyster-tongs the chiels did take
Dim grew the sight, and every blood-drop cold,
As knights in scarce romaunt, sung by the bards of old.

For not in daylight were their rites performed;
— When night-capped heads were on their pillow
laid,
Sleep-freed from biting care, by thought unharmed,
Snoring ere word was spoke, or prayer was said —
'T was then the mattock and the busy spade,
The pump, the bucket, and the windlass rope
In busy silence plied the mystic trade,

While resolution, beckoned on by hope,
Did sweat and agonize the sought-for chest to ope.

Beneath the wave, the iron chest is hot,
Deep growls are heard and reddening eyes are seen,
Yet of the Black Dog she had told them not,
Nor of the gray wild-geese with eyes of green,
That screamed, and yelled, and hovered close be-
tween
The buried gold and the rapacious hand.
Here should she be, though mountains intervene,
To scatter, with her crooked witch-hazle wand,
The wave-born sprites, that keep their treasure from
the land.

She cannot, may not come, the rotten wharf
Of mould'ring planks and rusty spikes is there,
And he who owned a quarter or a half
Is disappointed, and the witch is — where?
Vermont still harbours her — go seek her there,
The grandam of Joe Strickland — find her nest,
Where summer icicles and snowballs are,
Where black swans paddle and where petrils rest —
Symmes be your trusty guide, and Robert Kidd your
guest.

THE GNOME AND THE PADDOCK.

WHAT THE GNOME SAID TO THE PADDOCK IN A BLASTED ROCK.*

I AM a Gnome, and this old Granite ledge
My home and habitation, since the days
When the big floods brake up, and massy rain
Fell, deluge upon deluge, to the earth, —
When lightning, hot and hissing, crinkled by
Each scathed and thunder-blasted twig that showed
Its leaf above the waters. Years had passed,
And centuries too, when by this sheltered side
The Indian built his fire, and ate his samp,
And laid him down — how quietly — beneath
The shadow of this rock. 'T was great to him,
And in a weary land. For yonder, where
The school-boy flies his kite, and little girls
Seek four-leaved clover — there the Buffalo
Led his wild herd. There once, and only once,
The Mammoth stalked. Thou, Paddock, heard'st his
tread,

* A Paddock is a toad that lives in a rock.

But I, — I *saw* him. By this very rock —
This little ledge he passed. Three stately steps!
And every rough and wooded promontory
Trembled.

And for his voice — 't was musical,
And though too sonorous for human ear,
Yet to a Gnome 't was wondrous — exquisite ;
For every vein of undiscovered ore
Rang in full harmony to that bold tone.
From the wild surface to the lowest depth,
And through, and round the pillars of the earth,
Were silver streaks and golden radiants
That trembled through their courses, when a note
Congenial waked their low, sweet, solemn sound.

But hush thee, Paddock! Good-by once for all —
There comes old Burdick with an iron rod,
And near him, one who with a powder-flask
Will blow us both sky-high. Adieu, sweet vestal,
And when I meet you in a museum
Do not forget me dearest!

SONG.

THE rocks, the rocks, among the rocks
  My only lover lives ;
To me the plain, to me the main,
  Nor fear nor pleasure gives.

I love not in the sunny day
  To weed and till the ground,
While my wild lover far away,
  Hunts with his lazy hound.

Nor would I be a sailor's wife,
  Too far from me is he ;
For I must toil, and I must strive,
  While he is on the sea.

Give me a lover to my cheek,
  A husband to my arms,
Nor would I other dowry seek,
  Than hills and rocky farms.

The meadow's calms, the ocean's shocks,
  Each ruins or deceives;
The rocks, the rocks, among the rocks,
  My only lover lives.

ON THE DEATH OF AN OLD TOWNSMAN.*

Young he left thee, poor he left thee,
  Sad he left thee, Emerald Isle—
When oppression's cloud bereft thee
  Of thy last and saddest smile.

Here he came, but Ireland ever
  Warmed his heart and filled his thought—
Wandering son of Erin never
  Sought his hearth and found it not.

Fast by Liffey's lovely borders,
  Broad of wave and darkly deep,
Fast by Leixlip's leaping waters,
  Parents, friends, and kindred sleep.

* Attempted for the music of Rosseau's "Dream."

Here he dwelt, and all around him
  Blest his warm and honest heart —
Here he died as first we found him,
  Free from guile and void of art.

Touched but now with death's cold finger,
  Here he walks with us no more —
But if spirits ever linger,
  His will haunt the Liffey shore.

STANZAS.

How well I remember the paths that I trod
When a boy, with my bait and my light little rod ;
How eager I went, and how patient I stood,
  And felt not a bite through the whole afternoon ;
Wet, hungry, and tired, how, at sundown, I came,
The leaf it was green and the verdure the same,
But returning I found it so cold and so tame,
  'T was December to me, to the wood it was June.

I had dwelt where the lovely, the young, and the gay
Shed light on my path — but I went on my way,
My errand was fruitless, and tedious my stay,

And saddened I turned to the home of my youth;
Where now is the music, the life, and the glee —
There are smiles, there are dimples, — they are not for me,
And my faint, sickening spirit too plainly can see,
How warm was my fancy, how cold is the truth.

"IS IT FANCY, OR IS IT FACT?"

No more will I love, for my Mother is fled,
My Brother is gone to the seas for his bread,
And O, my poor Father by whom I am fed,
How cold is his hand when I take it.
He has cares, he has sorrows, and wild is his smile
When I strive all his harrowing thoughts to beguile ;
I gaze on his anguish, and fancy the while
That his heart wants but little to break it.

No more will I love — for my lover is gone,
At noonday the grasshopper sits by the stone,
And at twilight the whip-poor-will utters his moan
Where deep in the wood he is buried.
'T was there that he wished to be laid, for 't was there
That truth told its tale, and that love breathed its prayer,

And the heart taught the tongue a sad promise to
swear
That he and his love should be married.

He 's wedded to dust, and I 'm wedded to woe,
My Father's distracted, and where shall I go —
Should I follow my mother — O misery — no,
I am not, I am not her daughter.
One hope I can cherish — one form I can seek,
On one breast I can sigh, to one heart I can speak,
And the tear I next shed shall fall full on his cheek —
The brother that ventured the water.

ON A RAINBOW AT NIGHT.

The bow that spans the storm is beautiful;
Yet — how we view it! from our very cradle
E'en to the extreme of our most ripened wisdom
'T is treated as a toy. Philosophers,
With bits of glass and one small beam of light,
Make mimic rainbows upon college walls,
And lecture upon raindrops — how the light
Impinges, is refracted, bent and formed,
Ending with pious hintings to the class
With what analogies God's light is sent —
How mathematical his heavenly bow!

— The painter daubs it on his varnished cloth,
And with gamboge and verdigris, makes out
A tolerable rainbow — to be viewed,
Admired, and bought by folly's connoisseurs.
— As silly as the rest, the mother lifts
Her squalling child, whom rattle will not please,
Nor pap, nor coral with its silver bells,
To look upon the rainbow. — But too gross
Such gaze — and, folding up its heavenly robes,
"Like as a garment," on the meteor rolls.

"The Heavens shall pass away, as doth a scroll"—
Like as a scroll they stand. O! who that marked
That page of Heaven's bright book — when a new
light
Was broad upon his vision — (when the world
Turned from the sun, and the sun's worldly day)
But thought — all else forgot — but thought on Thee;
Nor painted — nor philosophized — nor smiled.

The sun is of our system, but the stars
Are set in Heaven. The day is made for man.
— At such a time — with such a gloried sky,
Even man feels that the *night* is made for God.

TO A FRIEND IN THE NAVY, SICK AT HOME.

The wave, the wave, the Yankee wave
That dances white and blue,
That roars in might, or laughs outright,
Or smiles and whispers too,
It is the same, whence'er it came,
And wheresoe'er it go, —
In piping gale or plaintive wail,
In triumph or in woe.

You 've seen it on mid-ocean's surge
When war called up its wrath,
Yelling the fated foeman's dirge,
And howling round his path, —
You 've seen it on the playful shore,
Its cheek upon the sand,
When winds were still and storms were o'er,
Kissing the quiet land.

By every promontory's sweep,
By every little bay,
By every shore and every steep
Where the smooth eddies play, —

Where'er the silver minim's fin
  Scoops out his tiny cave,
To paddle or to ponder in,
  You 've seen the Yankee wave.

How gayly did it once bear up
  Your little shingle boat,
And, when a bigger boy, on it
  Your skiff you first did float;
And since, upon the broadest deck
  That ever swam the seas,
You 've raised a penon, proudest yet
  That ever flapped the breeze.

Soon may you leave your fevered bed,
  As one who quits a wreck,
And show once more a — —'s head
  Upon a quarter-deck, —
Yes! leave your home, for ocean's foam,
  And join your comrades brave,
For well I know, of all below,
  You love the Yankee wave.

THE SMACK RACE.

Are they not beautiful? how light they float,
  How gracefully they sit upon the wave!
The water buoys no surer, fleeter boat,
  None that will Ocean's danger better brave.
  Forget not too, that sea-washed barrens gave
A hardy race to man each brace and line,
  Warm hearted and hard handed — all they crave
  Is but to seek and search the boist'rous brine
Where winters have no sun, and north lights dimly
    shine.

Thames! on thy smiling harbour now
How dips and bends each lively bow,
    As pleased to wanton there.
And need they longer there to ride?
The time is come and fair the tide,
    The wind is fresh and fair.

Away! the peak is trimly set,
The jib with schoot-horn duly wet,

The trembling helm is true,
One glass of grog, one signal gun,
Three cheers for luck and one for fun, —
Which is the happier crew ?

Over the broad, the blue, the clear,
The noble harbour, on they steer
By every well known spot.
In sailor's heart, in sea-bird's cry,
In pilot's thought, in poet's eye,
When are such scenes forgot ?

I love them, for the porpoise plays
In all their bleached and pebbly bays,
And every haunt explores ; —
I love them, that the hardy breeze
Sweeps daily from the healthful seas,
Blessing the happy shores.

* * * * *

Now taughter brace the laboring boom,
Bring the lee gunwale to the foam
And haul the bonnet flat :
They have the freshest of the breeze —
They have the widest of the seas, —
"We 'll beat 'em for all that."

See ! the wild wind bears down the peak,
And shows its shear the garboard streak,

Loose is the leeward shroud;
The helm, a-weather, bears her round
That hard-sought, hard gained racing ground,
So elegantly proud.

And now, good luck my honest hearts,
Well do you bear your dangerous parts,
And well I wish you all:
I little know your terms of skill,
But you shall have my right good will,
Whatever chance befall.

Good wives on shore, good winds at sea,
Fishing enough where'er you be,
And very many bites;
Plenty of fish and children too,
Days well employed, and not a few
Of quiet, happy nights.

THE FOOT.

"Δὸς ποῦ στῶ, καὶ τὸν κόσμον κινήσω."

I SING the Foot. Let every Muse's wing
Arrange its quills and fan the classic lay —

For Phœbus had a foot — and Venus blessed
Had more than that, a foot and ancle too.
Neptune, as Homer sung, could cause the shades,
And woods, and mountains tremble with his step.
Immortal was his foot-fall. Juno bright,
Stampted, when she scolded forth in Jove's own
court.
'T was Hebe's foot that bore the nectar round,
And Jupiter's great toe that Mulciber
Leaped from to Lemnos. — But enough of all
This heathen lore — this pantheon exercise.

What when the drum beats, and the panting ranks
Are joining, closing, moving on the foe —
When the deep whisper speeds along the line,
And all must "do or die" — what onward moves
The heart-pulse and the nerve, the ready hand,
The eye determined, and the kindling soul!
What urges up the bayonet — what mounts
The desperate height, the ladder and the breach,
And tramples on the rended, blood-stained flag?

What firmest paces on the rampart walk,
Or softest trips it to a lady's bower,
Or lightest sports it in the fairy dance,
Or what, on provocation, first applies
Its energies to kick a scamp down stairs?

O swift Achilles of the tender heel —
O well-shod Grecians of the classic boots, —
O Infantry of poets, to whose feet
Nor boot, nor shoe, nor stocking e'er belonged,
O Cinderilla of the vitreous sock —
O Giant-killing Jack with seven leagued strides,
Assist me to immortalize the foot.

FORT GRISWOLD, SEPT. 6, 1781.

WHAT seek ye here — ye desperate band?
Why on this rough and rocky land,
With sly and muffled oar, —
Why in this red and bright array
Stealing along the fisher's bay
Pull ye your boats to shore?

Day broke upon that gentlest Sound
Sequestered, that the sea has found
In its adventurous roam,
A halcyon surface — pure and deep,
And placid as an Infant's sleep
Cradled and rocked at home.

What wakes the sleeper? Harm is near —
That strange rough whisper in his ear,

It is a murderer's breath;
A thousand bayonets are bright
Beneath the blessed morning's light,
Moving to blood and death.

Land ye and march — but bid farewell
To this lone Sound, its coming swell
May moan when none can save;
Many shall go, and few return,
That rock shall be your only urn,
That sand your only grave.

Across the river's placid tide,
With steady stroke is seen to glide
A little vent'rous boat:
'T was like the cloud Elijah saw,
Small as his hand, yet soon to draw
Its quivered lightnings out.

'T was like that cloud, for in it went
A heart to spend and to be spent
Till the last drop was shed;
'T was like that cloud, it had a hand
That o'er its loved, its native land
A shadow broad has spread.

Ledyard! thy morning thought was brave,
To fight, to conquer, and to save,
Or fearlessly to die;

Well didst thou hold that feeling true, —
Didst well that purpose bold pursue
Till death closed down thine eye.

I dare not tell in these poor rhymes
That bloody tale of butchering times —
'T is too well known to all;
I write not of the foeman's path,
I write not of the battle's wrath,
But of the Hero's fall.

He sleeps where many brave men sleep —
Near Groton heights — and nibbling sheep
Their grassy graves have found;
But some, they are a few, are laid
Beneath a little swarded glade
On Fisher's Island sound.

The Sound is peaceful now, as when
It saw that armed array of men;
And one old fisher there
Gave me this tale — 't was he who told
The rough, the headlong, and the bold,
How their rash fight should fare.

He too is dead; and most are dead
Who stood or fell, who fought or fled
On that September day.

Old man! thy bones are gently laid
Close by yon shattered oak tree's shade,
  Beside the fisher's bay.

I KNOW A BROOK.

I KNOW a brook that winds its way along
A dull and stony margin — dwarfish trees
And barren vegetation mark its course.
The stern, bold grandeur of the granite rock
Frowns not upon it — and the smooth, green lawn
Slopes not to meet it. Nothing there is seen
Save one pure limpid spring, perennial,
That oozes from the rock and from the moss.
There, all that flourishes of bright and green
Is clustered, there the freshest of the grass
Laves in the welling rill. No man would think
In such a cold and barren spot, to find
Any thing sweet, or pure, or beautiful;
But yet, I say, it is the loveliest gush
—'T is so sequestered, and so arboured o'er
With nature's wildness in its summer glow —
The loveliest gush that ever spouted out
Upon my wandering path. Through mud and mire,
O'er many a bramble, many a jagged shoot

I stumbled, ere I found it. There I placed
A frail memorial — that, when again
I should revisit it, the thought might come
Of the dull *tide of life*, and that pure spring
Which he who drinks of never shall thirst more.

THE DROWNED BOY.

Sad was the lot, sad was the tale
  Of him who lies unconscious here ;
His locks are lifted by the gale,
No mourner comes his loss to wail,
  No friend to wait upon his bier.

I 've seen him in some lonely hour
  Gazing upon the bright blue sky,
And though the black'ning cloud might lour,
Careless he 'd view the coming shower,
  Nor heed the storm that muttered by.

Sad did he seem for one so young,
  'T was in a bitter mood he smiled,
And as he paced the path along,
He had a strange and wayward song,
  And gestured to his measure wild.

Whether 't was want or cruelty
  That caused his mind thus wild to rove,
Or whether to his boyish eye,
His fancy gave the madd'ning joy,
  Of ceaseless, hopeless, idle love,

I know not, — but he never slept,
  Upon a quiet, peaceful bed;
He to himself his vigils kept,
None but himself for him has wept,
  None mourn him now that he is dead.

THE WIDOWER.

O doth it walk — that spirit bright and pure,
And may it disembodied, ever come
Back to this earth? I do not, dare not hope,
A reappearance of that kindest eye,
Or of that smoothest cheek or sweetest voice, —
But can she see my tears, when I, alone,
Weep by her grave? and may she leave the throng
Where angels minister and saints adore,
To visit this sad earth!

When, as the nights
Of fireside winter gather chilly round,

I kiss our little child, and lay me down
Upon a widowed pillow, doth she leave
Those glorious, holy, heavenly essences,
Those sacred perfumes round the throne on high,
To keep a watch on me? and upon ours?
—Her I did love, and I was loved again,—
And had it been *my* mortal lot, instead,
I would, were I accepted, ask my God,
For one more look upon my wife and child.

SATURDAY NIGHT AT SEA.

It is well known, that naval officers, as well as their seamen, appropriate Saturday night, at sea, to the subject of their "*domestic relations*," over a glass of wine, or of grog, as the case may be. It may not be so notorious, that their female friends drink salt water in celebration of this nautical vigil.

A MOTHER stood by the pebbled shore,
In her hand she held a bowl—
"Now I 'll drink a draught of the salted seas
That broadly to me roll!—
On them I have an only son,
Can he forget me quite?
O! if his week away has run,
He 'll think of me this night.

And may he never on the track
Of ocean in its foam,
Fail to look gladly — kindly back
To those he left at home.
I pledge him in the ocean brine,
Let him pledge me in ruddy wine."

A sister stood where the breakers fall
In thunders, on the beach,
And out were stretched her eager arms,
For one she could not reach.
"I 'll dip my hand, my foot, my lip,
Into the foaming white,
For sure as this sand the sea doth sip
He 'll think of me this night.
And may he never, on the deck,
Or on the giddy mast,
In gale or battle, storm or wreck,
Forget the happy past.
I pledge him in the ocean brine,
Let him pledge me in ruddy wine."

A wife went down to the water's brink,
And thither a goblet brought;
"Here will I drink, and here I 'll think
As once we two have thought.
We 've romped by rock, and wood, and shore,
When moon and stars were bright,

And he, where'er the tempests roar,
Will think on me this night.
And may he ever, ever meet
With a friend as true and kind,
But not to night shall he forget
The wife he left behind.
I sip for him the ocean brine,
He 'll quaff for me the ruddy wine.

A maid came down with a hasty foot —
"My lover is far at sea,
But I 'll fill my cup, and I 'll drink it out
To him who deserted me.
Nor mother, nor sister, nor wife, am I,
His careless heart is light —
And he will neither weep, nor sigh,
Nor think of me, this night; —
He will, HE WILL, a *Sailor's* heart
Is true as it is brave,
From home and love 't will no more part
Than the keel will quit the wave.
I pledge thee, Love, in ocean's brine,
Pledge gayly back in ruddy wine."

EPISTLE FROM ONE ABSENT EDITOR TO ANOTHER.

Subscribers to ye! J. T. B.
Where'er ye flit, where'er ye flee —
And though ye 'll na remember me
        In your braw lodgin,
I trust ye 'll ha'e the grace to see
        Friends wi'out dodgin.

O gin I were in stage or boat,
Wi' stuffed valise and dapper coat,
How blithely wad I ride or float
        On land an' water;
But here I am, na worth a groat —
        'T is nae great matter.

I hope, dear sir, it winna vex ye
To hear I *borrow* the Galaxy,
Wherein ye rave at sic as tax ye
        Wi' a that loss —
But dinna let thae things perplex ye,
        And be na cross.

I ken ye 're crouse, and gi'e sma' glint
At rhyme, when there 's nae meaning in 't,
And sae, my verse I weel may stint
For a' *you* read on 't;
And my puir muse begins to hint
There 's little need on 't.

I only meant to let ye ken
That I, like ither absent men,
Have not been busy at my pen
In Hartford City,
But only scribbled now and then —
"The mair 's the pity."

I greet thee frae the banks and braes
That saw me in my childish days,
Where neither sylphs nor pranking fays
Buttoned my jacket;
The nearest *I* saw, in my strays,
Was auld Till Becket.

May you, by Tiber's favored burn,
Or where Potomac sees the urn
That patriot-poets stop and turn
To make a verse on,
Or 'mid the rigs o' Southern corn,
Meet nae worse person.*

* In a note to one of Burns' sweetest songs, "The Land

[AN INVOCATION.

O DEATH! O grave! O endless world beyond!
And Thou, the Holy One, that shuttest up
What no man openeth, — that openeth
That which nor man — nor death — nor the filled grave
Can ever shut? To Thee, how reverend,
How humble, and how pure should be our prayer.
Forgive us, for what are we! What but worms
That crawl, and bask, and shine — then writhe and die·
But there is hope in Heaven. I hear a voice
That says the dead are blessed, if they die
In Him who died for them. That whoso lives
Believing, shall not die eternally.
— So may we live, and so apply our hearts
To God's true wisdom in our numbered days,

o' the Leal"— republished in the Mirror a few months before the above was written — Brainard says, — "It may show what too few understand, that nobody can write a real Scottish song but a Scotchman. Bad spelling, misapplied provincialisms, and cockney sensibility, will never pass as the production of Allan Cunningham or Robert Burns."

That though we be cut down even as the flowers,
And though we flee like passing shadows by,
Hereafter we may bloom again, — and stand
Where all that blooms shall bloom eternally,
And shadows, like the bitter thoughts of life,
Can never flit across the holy path,
Nor darken one forgiving smile of Heaven.

CHARITY.

Sweet Charity! thou of the kindest voice,
Of lightest hand, of softest — meekest eye,
And gentlest footstep, making but the noise
Of a good angel's pinions floating by,
Go forth! but not to dwellings where the sigh
Of poverty and wretchedness is heard,
Not to the hovel, nor the human sty,
Where conscience, O! how burningly, is seared,
Where Heaven is scarcely known, and Hell but little
feared.

Sweet spirit, Go not there. There thou hast been,
And seen, nor pity, nor relief bestowed

By woman's eye, nor by the hand of men,
On them who bear such miserable load ;
What votary hast Thou, at their abode ?
What kind heart brings its tearful off'ring there,
And, grieved that 't is no more, lifts up to God
Its humble, earnest, holy, secret prayer,
Breathed mid the low and vile, in winter's midnight
air ?

Go to the rich, the gay, and the secure,
Bold be thy step, and heavy be thy hand,
Knock loud and long, at Fashion's partial door,
And swell thy voice to terror's bold command ;
And he, who builds upon extortion's sand,
He, of the purple and the linen fine,
Owner of widow's stock and orphan's land,
Shall shuddering turn from his untasted wine,
And feel, that to do well, his all he should resign.

Go to the lovely, not in sighing smiles,
At which the thoughtless fool might smiling sigh,
— Scatter her freaks, her follies, and her wiles,
With the stern beauty of religion's eye ;
Teach her the tear of grief — of shame to dry,
To drop on frailty meek compassion's balm,
To do aright — to feel aright — to try
Her envious, hateful passions first to calm ;
Then shed upon her soul, not on her face thy charm.

Go to yon Pharisee — the heartless wretch,
That prates of holiness, and hunts for sin,
For faults of others ever on the stretch,
All gaze without, and not one glance within ;
And worse, much worse, not one kind wish to win
A sinner back — but to detect, betray,
And punish. Go and tell him to begin
Anew — and point him to salvation's way,
The sermon on the mount to us poor sons of clay.

Touch not their gold, but touch —*Thou canst*— their heart,
For there be many, who, with open purse,
Will greet thee in that market-place, their mart
Of cold hypocrisy, or something worse :
Unkind and selfish — theirs may be the curse
" *Thy money perish with thee.*" Learn thou them,
Sweet Charity ! their *kindness* to disburse —
And Self's deep deadly current strong to stem ;
A sigh shall win a pearl — a tear a diadem.

How blessed are thy feet. Thy footsteps stray
From open paths, and seek a grass-grown track
Through shades impervious to the gaze of day ;
Onward flies light, a form that turns not back
At sight of chasm, or torrent never slack ;

Quiet and bold, and sure the errand speeds,
Nor doth the kindly deed a blessing lack —
To sorrow, joy — to anguish, peace succeeds,
The eye no longer weeps, the heart no longer bleeds.

ADDENDA.

The author, in revising his poems for the first edition, made many alterations of them as they originally appeared in the Mirror. As these changes may interest some of his readers, a few — the most important of them — follow; and to render them with perspicuity, the revised, with the original readings are given — the latter being italicized.

MATCHIT MOODUS.

Ere a star can wink, the time, and the place,
  And the seat, —
Ere the star that falls can run its race,
  The seat of the earthquake's power.

ON THE DEATH OF COMMODORE PERRY.

A bolder bard may choose a loftier name, —
Another hand may choose another theme,
May sing of Nelson.

THE SHAD SPIRIT.

The Shad Spirit holds his onward course,
With the flock that his whistle calls.
With the flocks which his whistle calls.

And who can tell him the fated time, —
And well can he tell the fated time
To undertake his task.

Though the wind is light, the wave is white
With the fleece of the flock that 's near;
And he sweeps on high, like the scud of the sky, —
The wind is light, and the wave is white,
With the fleece of the flock that 's near;
Like the breath of the breeze, he comes over the seas,
And faithfully leads them here.

Then carry the nets to the river's shore, —
So carry the nets to the nearest shore,
And take what the Shad Spirit brings.

ON THE BIRTHDAY OF WASHINGTON.

O send back the soul that can stand where he stood, —
O send back a form that shall stand as *he* stood,
Unsubdued by the tempest, —

LINES SUGGESTED BY A LATE OCCURRENCE.

And from a mother's silence I shall learn, —
And from a mother's holiest look, shall learn
A parents thanks to God, —

And shall I see again
The look of kindness as when, —
O! I shall see again
That same kind look I saw, when last we met.

That dark stream below!
Like time it knows no ebb, till it has ceased to flow.
May peace be in its ebb — there 's ruin in its flow.

THE GUERRILLA.

And at its front we 'll be the first,
To go with it to war.
And with it go to war.

ON THE LOSS OF A PIOUS FRIEND.

Hope in your mountains, and hope in your streams,
Bow lowly to them, and, —
Bow down in their worship, and loudly pray.

THE END.

www.ingramcontent.com/pod-product-compliance
Lightning Source LLC
LaVergne TN
LVHW010252110826
845151LV00004B/1449

* 9 7 8 1 4 2 5 5 2 2 7 2 8 *